The Native Hawaiian Government Reorganization Act of 2005

A Briefing Before
The United States Commission on Civil Rights
Held in Washington, D.C., January 20, 2006

Briefing Report

U.S. Commission on Civil Rights
The U.S. Commission on Civil Rights is an independent, bipartisan agency established by Congress in 1957. It is directed to:

- Investigate complaints alleging that citizens are being deprived of their right to vote by reason of their race, color, religion, sex, age, disability, or national origin, or by reason of fraudulent practices.

- Study and collect information relating to discrimination or a denial of equal protection of the laws under the Constitution because of race, color, religion, sex, age, disability, or national origin, or in the administration of justice.

- Appraise federal laws and policies with respect to discrimination or denial of equal protection of the laws because of race, color, religion, sex, age, disability, or national origin, or in the administration of justice.

- Serve as a national clearinghouse for information in respect to discrimination or denial of equal protection of the laws because of race, color, religion, sex, age, disability, or national origin.

- Submit reports, findings, and recommendations to the President and Congress.

- Issue public service announcements to discourage discrimination or denial of equal protection of the laws.

Members of the Commission
Gerald A. Reynolds, *Chairperson*
Abigail Thernstrom, *Vice Chairperson*
Jennifer C. Braceras
Peter N. Kirsanow
Arlan D. Melendez
Ashley L. Taylor
Michael Yaki

Kenneth L. Marcus, *Staff Director*

U.S. Commission on Civil Rights
624 Ninth Street, NW
Washington, DC 20425

(202) 376-8128 voice
(202) 376-8116 TTY
www.usccr.gov

Table of Contents

Executive Summary

On January 20, 2006, a panel of experts briefed members of the U.S. Commission on Civil Rights on the Native Hawaiian Government Reorganization Act of 2005. Noe Kalipi, the Democratic Staff Director on the Senate Committee on Veteran's Affairs; H. William Burgess, Lead Attorney, Grassroots Institute of Hawaii; H. Christopher Bartolomucci, Partner, Hogan & Hartson; and Gail Heriot, Professor of Law, University of San Diego Law School made presentations and offered their expertise. The briefing was held at the U.S. Commission on Civil Rights headquarters in Washington, D.C. A transcript of the briefing is available on the Commission's website, www.usccr.gov, and by request from Publications Office, U.S. Commission on Civil Rights, 624 Ninth Street, NW, Room 600, Washington, D.C. 20425, (202) 376-8128, publications@usccr.gov. The Commission received sixteen timely public comments from this briefing. Most of these comments were from individuals who oppose the legislation on the ground that it would be racially divisive. Comments supporting the legislation were received from the State of Hawaii's congressional delegation, the American Bar Association, the State of Hawaii's Office of Hawaiian Affairs and Department of Hawaiian Homelands, and a University of Colorado law professor.

This briefing addressed the Native Hawaiian Government Reorganization Act of 2005 (S. 147 and H.R. 309) proposed by Senator Daniel Akaka. The proposed legislation would:

- Recognize a right of the Native Hawaiian people to reorganize the Native Hawaiian governing entity to provide for their common welfare and to adopt appropriate organic governing documents;

- Establish a Commission to: (1) prepare and maintain a roll of the adult members of the Native Hawaiian community who elect to participate in such reorganization; and (2) certify that the adult members of the Native Hawaiian community proposed for inclusion on the roll meet the definition of Native Hawaiian, defined in the bill as either an individual "who is one of the indigenous, native people of Hawaii and who is a direct lineal descendant of the aboriginal, indigenous, native people who resided in the islands that now comprise the State of Hawaii on or before January 1, 1893; and occupied and exercised sovereignty in the Hawaiian archipelago, including the area that now constitutes the State of Hawaii" or an individual "who is one of the indigenous, native people of Hawaii and who was eligible in 1921 for the programs authorized by the Hawaiian Homes Commission Act or a direct lineal descendant of that individual";

- Outline the process for the reorganization, which includes forming a Native Hawaiian Governing Council;

- Reaffirm the political and legal relationship between the United States and the Native Hawaiian governing entity upon certification required by the Secretary regarding the organic governing documents and the election of the entity's officers;

- Extend Federal recognition to the governing entity as the representative governing body of the Native Hawaiian people; and

- Authorize the United States, upon the reaffirmation of such political and legal relationship, to enter into negotiations with the governing entity to lead to an agreement addressing specified matters, including the transfer of lands, natural resources, and other assets, and the protection of existing rights related to such lands or resources.

Previously, the Hawaii Advisory Committee to the Commission held community forums in August 1998 and September 2000 in which speakers addressed Congress' joint resolution apologizing to Hawaii for the alleged role of the United States in the overthrow of the Hawaiian monarchy and the *Rice v. Cayetano* decision by the United States Supreme Court, respectively. Information presented at these forums was later summarized in the Committee's 2001 report, *Reconciliation at a Crossroads.* This Committee had also issued a report, A *Broken Trust: The Hawaiian Homelands Program: Seventy Years of Failure of the Federal and State Governments to Protect the Civil Rights of Native Hawaiians,* in 1991 based on information presented in a 1988 public forum and 1990 factfinding meeting. This report examined the extent to which both the Federal government and the State of Hawaii were meeting their trust obligations to Native Hawaiians under the Hawaiian Homes Commission Act of 1921.

Noe Kalipi

Ms. Kalipi delivered testimony that was prepared and submitted by Patricia M. Zell in her capacity as former Staff Director and Chief Counsel of the Senate Committee on Indian Affairs. Ms. Kalipi argued in favor of Senate Bill 147, the Native Hawaiian Government Reorganization Act of 2005 (S.147). She explained that Native Hawaiians are aboriginal peoples, present in the United States prior to the formation of the American republic. Congress may deal with Native Hawaiians under the same constitutional authority that Congress deals with Native American communities. The relationship is one based not upon race, but instead upon political status as citizens of separate native polities incorporated within the United States.

The purpose of S.147 is to extend the federal policy of self governance and self determination to Native Hawaiians, providing parity in federal policies towards American Indians, Alaska Natives and Native Hawaiians. She explained that before the overthrow, the Kingdom of Hawaii was a distinct independent nation and a party to treaties with European nations and the United States. Unlike many other aboriginal peoples, the Native Hawaiians welcomed foreigners into their society. According to Ms. Kalipi, this generosity contributed to the overthrow of the monarchy, the establishment of a provisional government and the transfer of vast amounts of land to the United States. In her view, neither the fact that some non-natives were included in the Kingdom of Hawaii, nor the Kingdom's dissolution by a now apologetic U.S. government, makes the Kingdom non-native.

While Congress has enacted more than 160 statutes addressing the conditions of Native Hawaiians, the current ad hoc process fails to deal with Native Hawaiians as a sovereign entity. One example of the 160 statutes is the Hawaiian Homes Commission Act enacted by Congress in 1920 to establish protected lands for the Native Hawaiians who had been devastated by the overthrow. Others involve land rights and access to natural resources. Once self-governance has been properly recognized, Native Hawaiians would be able to set aside ad hoc processes and interact with the federal government in a more conventional government-to-government relationship.

She explained the structure of the bill, including the establishment of two independent processes. The first provides for a reorganization of the Native Hawaiian governing entity. Once reestablished as a sovereign entity, Hawaii's indigenous peoples could establish the criteria by which participation in the governing entity would be determined. The second is a negotiations process which provides that, upon federal recognition, the Native Hawaiian governing entity would be able to negotiate issues such as the transfer of any lands, natural resources and assets commensurate with jurisdiction; grievances for historical wrongs; and any governmental authority issues with the State of Hawaii and the United States. She explained that this negotiations process would be inclusive and was intended to represent all the people of Hawaii. Before any transfers could be completed, enabling legislation at the state and federal levels, if necessary, would be enacted.

She explained that efforts to preserve Native Hawaiian tradition, culture and custom are widely supported in Hawaii and are nonpartisan. The same sentiment carries over to S.147, which she said was supported by Hawaii's congressional delegation, the Hawaii State legislature, the Governor of Hawaii and the National Congress of American Indians and the Alaska Federation of Natives.

William H. Burgess

Mr. Burgess expressed grave concern that S.147 would permanently segregate the state of Hawaii and its people. He articulated three primary reasons to strongly oppose passage of S.147.

- First, he explained that peoples of various races and ethnicities had been united under the Kingdom of Hawaii. S. 147 would break that unity.

- Second, he challenged the analogy to Native American tribes. He disputed that any analogous Native Hawaiian entity had ever existed.

- Third, he challenged the reference to President Grover Cleveland's remarks on U.S. participation in the overthrow of the Kingdom of Hawaii, citing the Morgan Report of 1894.

He began with a discussion of unity and equality in Hawaii. He explained that long before the establishment of the Kingdom of Hawaii in 1810, King Kamehameha brought non-natives onto his forces and into his family. Since then, non-natives have continued to intermarry, assimilate, and contribute to the social, economic and political life of Hawaii both as leaders in high positions and as ordinary citizens. He felt that the driving force behind S.147 was discrimination between citizens of the United States based solely on ancestry. He described several ways in which that unity would be disturbed. Each involved the distribution of privileges on the basis of race. He explained that Hawaii is the only state that gives homesteads restricted exclusively to people that are defined explicitly by race. He cited the definition of Native Hawaiians in the Hawaii Homes Commission Act, which encompasses any descendent with some part of the blood of the races inhabiting the Hawaiian Islands prior to 1778. Additionally, the Office of Hawaiian Affairs provides annual cash distributions of public land trust revenues to those satisfying the definition of Native Hawaiian. For emphasis, he explained the injustice of providing money and public resources to that group, at state expense, while public schools in Hawaii were crumbling. Moreover, these benefits did not flow only to the limited racial group of those with 50 percent or more Hawaiian ancestry, but also to people with even a drop of

Hawaiian blood.

As to the Indian tribe analogy used by supporters of S. 147, Mr. Burgess disputed the basis upon which Native Hawaiians made a claim for parity with Native Americans. He disputed that Native Hawaiians were in fact identically situated to the Native Americans for whom recognition is granted. In his view, no group of Native Americans was recognized as a tribe simply because of ancestry. In each case, a longstanding political (not racial) entity was the subject of recognition. Conversely, he claimed that no Hawaiian tribe or government of any kind had existed for Native Hawaiians separate from the government of the rest of the citizens of Hawaii.

Finally, he disputed the claim that wrongdoing on the part of the United States government had played a role in the overthrow of Kingdom of Hawaii, as alleged in the Apology Resolution passed by Congress in 1893. For support, he relied upon the Morgan Report of February 26, 1894, an 800 page report of the Senate Committee on Foreign Affairs, which concluded that United States troops had landed as peacekeepers to protect American lives and property and had remained completely neutral. Based upon the Morgan Report, President Cleveland recognized the provisional government of Hawaii, and subsequently the Republic of Hawaii, as the lawful successor to the Kingdom of Hawaii, forever extinguishing claims of Native Hawaiians to the equivalent of tribal status.

H. Christopher Bartolomucci

Mr. Bartolomucci based his testimony on a memorandum he had coauthored with Georgetown University Law Center Professor Viet Dinh for the State of Hawaii's Office of Hawaiian Affairs. His remarks focused on Congress' power to enact S. 147. In his view, the principal legal question presented by S. 147 was whether Congress had the constitutional authority to treat Native Hawaiians in the same manner it treated other Native Americans. He found that constitutional text, Supreme Court precedent, and historical events provided the answer— Congress' broad power in regard to Indian tribes allows Congress to recognize Native Hawaiians as having the same sovereign status as the other indigenous peoples of this country.

He explained that Congress' broadest constitutional power, the power to regulate commerce, specifically encompasses the power to regulate commerce with the Indian tribes. He explained the two year old Supreme Court decision in *United States v. Lara*, where the Court held that "[t]he Constitution grants Congress broad general powers to legislate in respect to Indian tribes powers that we have consistently described as plenary and exclusive." Moreover, he identified one situation where Congress had used that broad power in the past to restore lost tribal sovereignty. In 1954, Congress terminated the sovereignty of the Menominee Indian Tribe in Wisconsin. In 1973, Congress reversed course and enacted the Menominee Restoration Act, which restored sovereignty to the Menominee Tribe.

Pointing to the Menominee Restoration Act, the Supreme Court in *Lara* affirmed that the Constitution authorized Congress to enact legislation "recognizing the existence of Indian tribes and restoring previously extinguished tribal status." Similarly, before Hawaii became a state, the Kingdom of Hawaii was a sovereign nation recognized as such by the United States. In 1893, American officials and the United States military aided the overthrow of the Hawaiian monarchy. A century later, in 1993, Congress formally apologized to the Hawaiian people for United States involvement in this regime change. Now, S. 147 is patterned after the Menominee

Restoration Act and would do for Native Hawaiians what Congress had done earlier for the Menominee Tribe.

Anticipating opposing arguments, Mr. Bartolomucci concluded that S. 147 does not run afoul of the Supreme Court's 2000 decision in *Rice v. Cayetano*. *Rice* had ruled that the State of Hawaii could not limit the right to vote in a state election to Native Hawaiians. *Rice* did not address whether Congress could treat Native Hawaiians as it treated other Native Americans. Indeed, the Court in *Rice* expressly declined to address whether Native Hawaiians have a status similar to Indians in organized tribes or whether Congress may treat the Native Hawaiians as it does the Indian tribes.

Some opponents of S. 147 have pointed to *Rice* in support of an argument that the bill violated the Equal Protection Clause. But Mr. Bartolomucci offered that the Supreme Court has long held that congressional legislation dealing with indigenous groups is political, not racial in character and is therefore neither discriminatory nor unconstitutional. Significantly, when Congress enacts laws for indigenous peoples it does so on a government-to-government basis. In fact, he reminded us, scores of federal laws and regulations exist relating to American Indians, Native Alaskans and Native Hawaiians, and none has ever been struck down as racially discriminatory.

In conclusion, Mr. Bartolomucci stated that a decision by Congress to treat Native Hawaiians like other native groups is a political decision, one that the courts are not likely to second-guess. The 1913 case of *United States v. Sandoval*, involving the New Mexico Pueblos, the Supreme Court ruled that Congress could treat the Pueblos as Indians even though their culture and customs differed from that of other Indian tribes. The Court decided that Congress' judgment was not arbitrary and that judicial review should end there. Mr. Bartolomucci opined that the different culture and customs of Native Hawaiians will likewise pose no barriers. Congressional action in S. 147 to treat Native Hawaiians differently is a political classification that is not arbitrary, and would therefore satisfy all constitutional requirements.

Gail Heriot

Ms. Heriot began by explaining the complexity of the body of Indian law and the presence of numerous contradictions. In her view, recognition of Native Hawaiians, an Indian megatribe, would be an unwelcome and major expansion to that body of law. Moreover, she felt that such an expansion would exceed Congress's constitutional authority.

First, she argued that the Constitution contains no clear statement of congressional authority to regulate existing Indian tribes as opposed to regulating commerce between the United States and Indian tribes. In her view, the power to authorize the creation of new tribes or even to authorize the reorganization of a previously existing tribe is not a regulation of commerce. She understood that the Commerce Clause must necessarily include some functions outside strictly commerce, but nevertheless felt that establishing tribes exceeded allowable non-commerce functions.

Additionally, Ms. Heriot disagreed with the reference made by Mr. Bartolomucci that Congress had reconstituted the Menominee Tribe. First, she explained that the purported termination and restoration of sovereignty was not challenged before the Supreme Court. The more important distinction was that the Menominee Tribe had not been extinguished by an act of Congress. Instead, federal supervision ceased as part of a general policy to decrease federal supervision over all Indian tribes. In contrast to Native Hawaiians, the tribe continued to exist; it continued to be organized as a corporation with the members of the tribe as shareholders of that corporation. Therefore, by recognizing the Menominee Tribe, Congress was not creating a tribe, nor was it establishing the mechanism to create a tribe. Congress simply recognized the tribe again and federal supervision was resumed.

She emphasized that there are standards for determining whether a group is a tribe. One important factor is that the political entity must exist continuously. No Native Hawaiian entity has existed continuously, as evidenced by the mechanism by which S.147 defines membership. A tribe that exists does not need to be told by the United States Government who is in the group and who is not.

Nevertheless, according to Ms. Heriot, another issue loomed larger. The State of Hawaii's Office of Hawaiian Affairs (OHA) currently administers a huge public trust for the benefit of all Hawaiians. In practice the trust provides benefits exclusively for ethnic Hawaiians, including special home loans, business loans, and housing and educational programs. The constitutionality of the current system has recently been called into question as a result of the Supreme Court's decision in *Rice v. Cayetano* and the Ninth Circuit's decision in *Doe v. Kamehameha Schools*, which is currently being reviewed by the Ninth Circuit *en banc*. Many expect other aspects of OHA's special benefits programs will be challenged in court on equal protection and other civil rights grounds. Ms. Heriot believes that S.147 is, in large measure, an effort to preserve that system.

In the *Rice* decision, the Supreme Court held that Hawaii's election system, under which only ethnic Hawaiians could vote for trustees of OHA, was a violation of the Constitution's Fifteenth Amendment, which prohibits discrimination on the basis of race in voting rights. In a later decision in the federal circuit courts, the *Doe* court held that the prestigious King Kamehameha Schools, which are privately run, cannot give ethnic Hawaiians priority over students of other races and ethnicities for admission without violating 42 USC Section 1981.

Ms. Heriot explained that the best hope for those who favor the current Native Hawaiian benefit programs is to transform them from programs that favor one race or ethnicity over others, to programs that favor members of a tribe over non-members. She found the basis for such an approach in *Morton v. Mancari*, a case involving a hiring preference for tribal members at the U.S. Bureau of Indian Affairs, where the Supreme Court provided that "such a benefit is granted to Indians not as a discreet racial group but rather as members of quasi-sovereign tribal entities." As Ms. Heriot explained, the *Mancari* decision, though, is a double-edged sword. If discrimination by the Bureau of Indian Affairs in favor of tribal members is not race-based, then presumably discrimination against tribal members by a state government is also not race-based. The very act of transforming ethnic Hawaiians into a tribe under S.147 would be an act performed on a racial group, not a tribal group. If it is done for the purpose of conferring very large benefits on that group, according to Ms. Heriot, then it would be an act of racial discrimination.

Discussion

Chairman Reynolds began the discussion summarizing key questions for the discussion period. He asked whether distributing benefits and burdens on the basis of race or ethnicity was constitutional. Assuming that it was constitutional, he then asked whether that practice was something we wanted to do or expand. Before opening the floor to questions from Commissioners, Chairman Reynolds permitted the panelists to provide any clarifying remarks that might have.

Mr. Bartolomucci began by explaining that in the *Lara* decision, Justice Breyer expressly stated that Congress had the authority to restore previously extinguished tribal status. In his view, that language clearly supported Congressional power to restore a tribe that had previously existed, as in the case of the Menominee. He added that he was not convinced that Native Hawaiians were not a continuously existing tribe. In his view, nothing that Congress or the federal government could do could take away their status or destroy their sovereignty. In response, Ms. Heriot distinguished the *Menominee* case from the Native Hawaiian situation by arguing that the Menominee Tribe did not disappear as a political unit. She referenced an unidentified case where, during the purportedly extinguished period, the Court recognized the sovereignty of the Menominee in the sense that they continued to be exempt from Wisconsin law on issues of fishing and hunting rights. However, if the Menominee continued to exist, then the case failed to establish precedence for restoration of Native Hawaiian sovereignty.

Commissioner Braceras asked about the preexistence of Native Hawaiian sovereignty and the role it played in any decision to grant or restore sovereignty. Ms. Kalipi explained that if our government had dissolved the Hawaiian monarchy, granting federal recognition would be a restoration of a preexisting native government—a restoration delayed only because an alternative form of government was forced upon the Hawaiian people. Mr. Burgess disputed her claim, arguing that the Kingdom of Hawaii had never been a tribe—it was never exclusively of, by or for Native Hawaiians. He cited the first constitution and the civil codes of the Kingdom of Hawaii, which provided that naturalized foreigners had the same rights, privileges, and immunities as natives. He also claimed that ethnic Hawaiians were a minority of the inhabitants of Hawaii in 1893. To his knowledge, non-natives played important roles as judges, elected officials in the legislature, and cabinet members and business leaders. Consequently, restoring the Kingdom would not mean creating an exclusively ethnic Hawaiian government, but would instead mean forming an inclusive government of all the people of Hawaii. His comments elicited questions about the definition of tribe and the definition of Native Hawaiian.

Explaining that Native Americans did not initiate the word "tribe," Commissioner Melendez asked for its definition, positing that what we now know as "Indian tribes" exercised self-governance in any number of ways. Ms. Heriot agreed that many groups called tribes have very different political structures. Nevertheless, she believed that the law required a continuous political unit recognizable as a political structure. To her knowledge, every federally recognized tribe had a continuous political structure. Any tribal political structure that might have existed for Native Hawaiians in the past did not exist anymore. She emphasized that Congress did not have the authority to recreate an extinguished political unit. Mr. Bartolomucci found it somewhat ironic that it was permissible to recognize Indian tribes that had been pushed off their lands and put into reservations, but that federal recognition was forbidden if the federal government had completely extinguished sovereignty.

Commissioner Taylor asked whether the key question was whether an identifiable structure existed at some point in time and whether an affirmative answer would imply that Congress was merely recognizing or restoring a sovereign entity, rather than creating one. He asked whether the sovereign entity had been extinguished when the monarchy was overthrown. Hearing that it had not, he asked whether it was accurate to say that sovereignty resided in the people. Ms. Kalipi explained that Native Hawaiians believe that the monarchy was their government. She explained that any differences between the Hawaiian concept of monarchy and either the Western concept of monarchy or the governing entity for other Native American tribes should not be held against Native Hawaiians.

Commissioner Braceras asked whether recognition of tribal status depended on the particular political history of the territory or whether it depended strictly on racial affiliation and cultural identification. Ms. Kalipi responded that it hinged upon both. The federal policy of self governance and self determination was based on the political and legal relationship that the United States had with the preexisting sovereign entity. It was impossible to separate the preexisting political entity from the culture that formed that political entity. Commissioner Yaki interjected that it was unreasonable to dispute that in Hawaii an indigenous sovereign government had been dissolved by the United States for its own purposes.

Mr. Burgess, with the support of Ms. Heriot, reminded the Commission that indigenous peoples have no status and effect under the Constitution. He stated that, in the *Rice* case, the Supreme Court failed to accept the argument that all indigenous people are entitled to a special relationship. He explained that the same argument had been made in *Arakaki v. State*. According to Mr. Burgess, the courts, for a second time, rejected arguments based on indigenous status. Although he acknowledged an international movement to declare the rights of indigenous people, he noted that it had not yet been adopted by the United States. In the *Rice* decision, he said, the Court found that defining Native Hawaiians based on ancestry, was simply creating a proxy for race. Similarly, he believed that using ancestry instead of race in S.147 was impermissible racial discrimination.

Commissioner Taylor asked whether recognizing a unique status for all indigenous people would be required if S.147 were to pass. Ms. Kalipi thought not. She explained that Congress had passed more than 160 laws and statutes to address the conditions of Native Hawaiians. Congress had previously established a political and legal relationship with Native Hawaiians dating back to 1893. This bill would simply formalize that political and legal relationship.

Commissioner Taylor recognized the significance of the federal government choosing to deal with Native Hawaiians as a group, but he nevertheless asked why the government chose not to deal with other indigenous groups. Commissioner Yaki suggested that the federal government's action toward Native Hawaiians was a half-hearted attempt to provide some sort of recognition to the fact that our actions in the Hawaiian Islands were improper. He saw S.147 as a simple method of completing the process of creating federal recognition of Native Hawaiians, a process that had been neglected since 1893.

Vice Chair Thernstrom asked for further clarification on whether the government in place in 1893 had been a government exclusively of Native Hawaiians. Ms. Kalipi acknowledged that it had not been. She explained that only about 40 percent of the Kingdom was ethnically Hawaiian. She reported that Native Hawaiians were the majority of people participating in what was still their government. She emphasized that a sovereign entity had the power to make its own decision as to how foreigners would participate. That the government had a mechanism to include foreigners did not make that government non-native. At this point Vice Chair Thernstrom asked whether it was appropriate to establish a new government that would have the ability to choose not to admit foreigners. Ms. Kalipi responded that the self-governing process would allow Native Hawaiians to decide if they wanted to admit foreigners or not. Making those decisions was consistent with the federal policy of self governance and self determination for indigenous peoples.

Several Commissioners and panelists saw reason to distinguish Native Hawaiians from Native Americans. Chairman Reynolds asked whether the different history and relationship with the U.S. government for Hawaiians would justify different treatment. Commissioner Yaki responded that refusing to call Native Hawaiians tribes for purposes of the Commerce Clause and the Treaty Clause was not reading history correctly. Commissioner Braceras disagreed, adding that constitutional and legal questions require that you deal with the text as written. She maintained that tribes did not necessarily include indigenous peoples.

Commissioner Melendez commented that fears of secession were unfounded and pointed out that Indian tribes would not be permitted to separate from the Union and neither would Native Hawaiians. He went on to state that under the Akaka bill Congress would retain control and could act to protect the civil rights of U.S. citizens. He then asked the panelists to compare the situation facing Native Hawaiians to that faced over the years by Native Americans. He concluded by stating that while it is impossible to right every wrong, some wrongs can and should be corrected. Ms. Heriot explained that she had no objection to the status of Indians in the United States. She distinguished Native Hawaiians by the many years during which nothing approaching a tribal entity existed in Hawaii. In her view, there is currently no functioning tribe. Rather than recognizing Indian tribes in the United States, Congress is seeking to create a mechanism that would allow a tribe to be created.

The concept of creating a tribe was also questioned from the perspective of race. Commissioner Taylor was the first to ask whether this bill merely created a racial or ethnically based group. He asked whether this group of indigenous peoples needed to have a recognized political system in place in order for this bill to be viable. Ms. Kalipi explained that the bill did not create a tribe, nor a group distinguished solely on race. Instead she explained that before 1893 Native Hawaiians had a political entity in place. With respect to any interim governing body after the overthrow, she explained that Hawaiians did the best they could without a government as others would perceive a government. She believed that S.147 would correct that injustice by reorganizing a recognizable government of indigenous peoples, not by creating a tribe.

Chairman Reynolds questioned the mechanism for selecting group membership. He asked whether it would work exactly like racial preferences in that the governing entity would have the ability to treat non-Native Hawaiians differently. Ms. Kalipi did not answer the question directly, instead clarifying that S.147 was based on the political and legal relationship that the United States has had with Native Hawaiians as an indigenous group, dating back to the relationships with a preexisting government. She also explained that S.147 defined Native Hawaiian for the sole purpose of identifying who can participate in the reorganization of the government.

This exchange prompted Commissioner Kirsanow to ask whether discrimination statutes and/or sovereign immunity would apply to the newly created sovereign governing entity if S.147 were to pass. Ms. Kalipi explained that the bill as currently amended would include sovereign immunity provisions. With respect to the anti-discrimination legislation, she explained that the organic governing documents created by the commission are required to provide for the protection of the civil rights of the citizens of the governing entity and all persons affected by the exercise of governmental powers and authorities by the Native Hawaiian governing entity... She further stated that the Secretary of the Interior has approval power of the organic governing documents and is tasked with ensuring that civil rights protections are included. If the Secretary of the Interior found the organic governing documents to be unsatisfactory, she could decline to certify the entity and provide federal recognition.

Vice Chair Thernstrom asked about the difference between a racial group and a tribal group if the tribal group was defined by "one drop of blood." Mr. Burgess and Ms. Heriot explained that membership in the group would be for lineal descendants of the indigenous peoples, not based on residence on the island.

Commissioner Yaki rephrased an earlier question on whether this bill would be divisive. Ms. Kalipi responded that she did not believe the bill would be divisive. She explained that almost every elected official in the State of Hawaii had come out in support of the bill. She also explained that the bill provides a structured process to finally allow the people of Hawaii, native and non-native, to begin to discuss the longstanding issues resulting from the overthrow of the Kingdom of Hawaii. She referenced the frequency of misunderstandings and the widespread mistrust prevalent throughout the islands. She explained that there would be no immediate transfer of land if this bill was enacted. First, the governing entity would need to be reorganized. Second, the federal government would need to be satisfied that all requirements were met before federal recognition would be granted. Subsequently, the governing entity would be able to negotiate any proposed transfer of lands and authority to the governing entity. Before any transfer could take place, enabling legislation at the federal and state levels would need to be passed.

Similarly, Commissioner Kirsanow asked how Native Hawaiians would be defined. Mr. Bartolomucci answered that the bill would not define membership in the Native Hawaiian entity. It would merely define the initial role of persons eligible to vote for an interim governing council. He explained the well established principle of Indian law that a tribe may decide who holds membership in the tribe. He also explained that the bill called for the Secretary of the Interior to create a commission of experts to determine Native Hawaiian ancestry and lineal descent. That commission would be responsible for establishing criteria for those able to vote for the governing entity and deciding whether individuals fall within that definition. Once membership is established, an initial election would determine an interim council. Later in the process, Native Hawaiians would decide who should be in the entity and how to define membership.

Ms. Heriot explained that the most worrisome aspects of the proposed legislation were already in place. OHA already manages a huge program of special benefits based on Hawaiian ethnicity. This bill simply recasts those benefits that already exist in terms that are not based specifically on race. Commissioner Yaki asked whether we would still have those concerns if these benefits were given by a sovereign tribal government, whether or not the sovereignty was continuous. Ms. Heriot explained that if the group had existed before, then it would not be a group that the United States is recognizing based on race. They would be recognized on the basis of existing sovereignty. Nevertheless, she disagreed that Native Hawaiians had sovereignty, because the law required that sovereignty be continuous. She insisted that Congress could not hand sovereignty to Native Hawaiians and then confer benefits based on that sovereignty.

Commissioner Taylor expressed his agreement with the importance allotted self determination of peoples as they relate to governing bodies, but questioned how additional groups could be recognized without advocating separation form the United States. Ms. Kalipi amplified her remarks on the purpose of S.147 by reminding the Commissioners that the federal government already has a federal policy of self-governance and self-determination with respect to some groups. Commissioner Yaki added that the structure provided by the government to provide recompense for actions taken by the government, such as the Hawaii Homes Commission, had only partially given the Native Hawaiians a feeling of control and autonomy over the decisions that were made. Concessions had not been obtained through a government-to-government relationship, as they had been for American Indian tribes or other sovereign nations. He emphasized that wanting to re-establish a government-to-government relationship did not mean that Native Hawaiians were not Americans. Responding to a question from Chairman Reynolds as to whether recompense meant reparations, Commissioner Yaki explained that the government had already initiated programs with Native Hawaiians; they had simply not done so in a manner that respects self-governance and self-determination. Ms. Kalipi echoed those remarks, declaring that S.147 was not about reparations. It was completely about process and the relationship between sovereign governments.

Commissioner Braceras asked whether the United States would want to perpetuate a system whereby certain groups were treated differently than others. Mr. Bartolomucci responded that Native Hawaiians should be treated the same as Native Alaskans or American Indians. He thought that self-governance could be expanded to Native Hawaiians with some justice. Several Commissioners asked whether other groups of people could make similar arguments for obtaining rights through self-governance programs. In light of the high intermarriage rate for Native Hawaiians and recognizing that Hawaii joined the United States in 1959 with an overwhelming vote, Vice Chair Thernstrom questioned whether further separation of Native Hawaiians was a good thing.

Commissioners Kirsanow and Braceras asked what had precipitated this legislation, how this legislation would make the situation better for Native Hawaiians and why the current state of affairs was inequitable. Ms. Heriot explained that this legislation was connected to the *Rice v. Cayetano* decision. In her view, the legislation was focused on providing an alternate justification for the racial preference system that is operated by OHA. Ms. Kalipi explained that the purpose of S.147 was to allow the people of Hawaii to move forward as a state by providing a structured process to allow Native Hawaiians to deal with the longstanding issues of the overthrow such as mistrust and misunderstanding. She explained further that federal policies of self-governance and self-determination allow indigenous peoples to have greater autonomy over their own natural resources and assets. Hawaii is the homeland for Native Hawaiians. Others had come in and taken over the homeland, at least partly due to federal policy. Protecting what Native Hawaiians currently have and restoring what had been lost requires that the current legal and political relationship be formalized.

Staff Director Marcus asked the panelists whether any of the concerns about the bill would be addressed by a potential amendment that could ensure that membership in the governing entity would not be based on racial characteristics, but on lineal descent from persons who lived in Hawaii at a particular time regardless of racial characteristics. Mr. Burgess thought that a substitute could not be used. He explained that establishing criteria based upon living at a particular place at a particular time had been held to be a proxy for race. He believed that the language used in S.147 to define ancestry was similar to the definition criticized by the *Rice* court. Ms. Heriot agreed that ancestry was often simply a proxy for race. Nevertheless, she thought that more information was required to answer the question. If the bill were amended such that group membership was defined in terms of ancestry as of 1775 she thought it would be simply a proxy for race. On the other hand, if the group were defined based on ancestry as of 1890, many people would be included who were not ethnically Hawaiian. So, she believed that such an amendment would satisfy the *Rice* test, though she remained concerned that the bill might still raise other constitutional issues.

Public Comments

The Commission voted to hold the record of the briefing open until March 21, 2006 to receive additional comments from the public. Sixteen such comments were received during that period. Most of these commenters wrote to express their opposition to the legislation, mainly on the ground that it would, in their view, formalize racially discriminatory practices. The State of Hawaii's Congressional Delegation, the State of Hawaii's Office of Hawaiian Affairs and Department of Hawaiian Homelands, and the American Bar Association each wrote to express their support. One commenter wrote to assuage concerns about the constitutionality of the proposed legislation.

While most commenters oppose the legislation, the governmental and institutional commenters primarily support it. For example, the Hawaii congressional delegation, as principal sponsors of the legislation, noted that they are "joined in support for this initiative by virtually all of Hawaii's other elected leaders, including, Governor Linda Lingle, [Hawaii's] State Legislature, and OHA, as well as virtually all of the principal national organizations representing American Indians and Alaskan Natives, and most recently the American Bar Association." The delegation also argued that there was "no question that the Akaka bill falls directly within the plenary power of Congress under our Constitution to establish national policy with respect to and behalf of our indigenous peoples." Similarly, the State of Hawaii's Department of Hawaiian Home Lands supports the legislation because it believes that the legislation would provide Native Hawaiians an "opportunity to manage and made decisions that impact their lands and their political and cultural identity." The American Bar Association presented their recently adopted policy supporting "the right of Native Hawaiians to seek federal recognition of a governing entity similar to that which many American Indians and Alaskan Natives currently enjoy."

These supporters of the legislation took great pains to analogize the situation of Native Hawaiians with those of Native Americans. For example, Charles Wilkinson, Professor of Law at the University of Colorado, argued that the "the right of self-determination and self-governance" of Native Hawaiians is premised upon "the sovereignty of America's indigenous, native people, " as opposed to other groups "defined by reference to their race of ethnicity." Similarly, the State's Office of Hawaiian Affairs stated that America's indigenous, native people are not defined by race or ethnicity, but "by the fact that their indigenous, native ancestors exercised sovereignty over the lands and areas that subsequently became part of the United States." Likewise, the State's Department of Hawaiian Home Lands believes that the proposed legislation "advances the Congress' intent to treat Native Hawaiians as a political body, not a racial group." The State of Hawaii's Congressional delegation argued that the legislation was needed to address the "ramifications of the overthrow of the Kingdom of Hawaii…[which] continue[s] to reverberate throughout our state and our communities…"

Finally, supporters of the legislation attempted to allay any fears of racial balkanization or equal protection violations. The State's Congressional delegation pointed out that the proposed legislation only "outlines steps through which federal recognition may be extended, "leaving the negotiation and implementation of its provisions to "subsequent mutual agreements by Congress, our executive branch, the State of Hawaii, and the reorganized Native Hawaiian entity." The American Bar Association argued that "Native Hawaiians, in seeking rights and privileges that other indigenous peoples of the United States enjoy under our legal system, are not compromising the rights of others but exercising their own rights…"

On the other hand, the great majority of commenters wrote to express their opposition to the legislation. Many of these comments argued, in very personal terms, that the proposed legislation would be inconsistent with basic American principles of equality, traditional Hawaiian values, and their own personal ethics. In the words of one commenter, the legislation would "enshrine racial discrimination into law." Some of these commenters stressed their own ethnic heritage, including Native Hawaiian ancestry, and argued that the legislation would be an affront both to their own personal identities and to those of their family members who lack Native Hawaiian blood. While space limitations preclude separate discussion of each letter, the following excerpts provide a representative sample of these statements:

- "As a person born and raised in Hawaii, of mixed parentage, I have always been proud of the color-blind nature of my homeland. My family includes people of every race, creed and color, including native Hawaiian as defined by the Akaka bill. The thought that portions of my family should be treated differently because of their genetic ancestry is anathema to me, and I beg you to oppose the Akaka bill, which would enshrine racial discrimination into law…The constitution of the Hawaiian Kingdom in 1840 declared that all men were "of one blood." Throughout the history of the Kingdom, the Republic, the Territory and the State of Hawaii, we have been a multi-racial and multi-cultural society. To separate out only those who had ancestors pre-1778, and take away from them their history of racial equality, their history of civil rights, and demand that they must govern themselves separately because of race, is an insult to the history of all the peoples of the islands of Hawaii. It would be just as reasonable to turn back the clock on civil rights in the mainland United States, and insist that whites must govern themselves, and blacks must govern themselves – separate but equal all over again!..." Jere Krischel

- "…It is appropriate to say that I am of Hawaiian, Caucasian and Chinese descent only because it shall be noted that I am a descendent of the indigenous peoples of Hawaii and do

13

not support the Akaka bill…If [the Akaka bill] comes to pass, I will no longer acknowledge my Hawaiian heritage as I will be forced to choose on which side of the fence to stand. I will choose the Anglo-American tradition of the right to life, liberty, property and the pursuit of happiness. This will prevent me from recognizing all that is Hawaiian in me. I consider the Akaka bill to be a proposal to violate my rights…" Kaleihanamau Johnson (Aiea, HI)

- "…I am writing to ask for the civil rights commission to oppose the Akaka Bill on the grounds that it will divide our state among racial lines…I am of native American blood (Nez Pierce Indian) but cannot be considered eligible for benefits such as those desired by native Hawaiians…The Akaka Bill will destroy our way of life in Hawaii…" Garry P. Smith (Ewa Beach, HI)

- "…I am a descendant of both: Kamehameha the Great, who united the islands and people, natives and non-natives and made Hawaii a model for the world: and the Mayflower pilgrims whose ideals of individual freedom and responsibility and self-reliance shaped the most inclusive and widely shared system of government in history: American democracy…The Akaka Bill would dishonor the unity and equality envisioned by Kamehameha the Great and the ideal of one nation, indivisible, composed of indestructible states, envisioned by the U.S. Constitution…" Rubellite Kawena Kinney Johnson (Honolulu, HI)

Other commenters argued that the legislation is a form of "racial balkanization," that it would harm the majority of Hawaiians, and that it would serve as a dangerous precedent to claims by other ethnic groups in the United States. Some commenters also attributed base motivations to the legislation's supporters.

The Commission considered and was informed by the full range of views expressed in its public briefing; written and oral statements provided by the panelists in support of and in opposition to the legislation; the work of the Commission's Hawaii State Advisory Committee, including its formal reports; and all public comments timely received in response to the Commission's public briefing, including comments from U.S. Senators, Congressmen, state officials, non-profit organizations and associations, and interested individuals. The Commission gratefully acknowledges the participation of countless individuals in this process, including participants from Hawaii, in Washington, D.C., and from other parts of the country.

Recommendation

The Commission recommends against passage of the Native Hawaiian Government Reorganization Act of 2005 (S. 147) as reported out of committee on May 16, 2005, or any other legislation that would discriminate on the basis of race or national origin and further subdivide the American people into discrete subgroups accorded varying degrees of privilege.

Briefing on the Native Hawaiian Government Reorganization Act before the United States Commission on Civil Rights
Gail Heriot

Indian law—that body of federal law that governs the allocation of authority over matters affecting Indians among the federal government, the state governments and the various tribal governments—is not generally beloved by those who like law to be logical and tidy. It suffers from generation after generation of shifting policies. As a result of this constant flux, the law's contradictory foundations render it very nearly incoherent. Are tribal governments separate sovereignties whose powers are inherent in that status? If so, once a tribal government is recognized, is not the United States obliged to recognize and defer to those inherent powers regardless of whether they are exercised in a manner that adheres to federal law or the Constitution? Alternatively, do tribes derive their powers by federal delegation? If so, aren't those powers completely subject to the Constitution? Can the powers be both inherent and delegated? And if some powers are inherent and others are delegated, which powers are inherent and which are delegated?

As I have suggested, the answers to these questions have important ramifications. At one extreme, if tribes are essentially foreign sovereign entities, their existence does not depend on Congressional legislation and dealing with them is mainly a matter for the President through his treaty power—which is precisely how the federal government did indeed treat them during the earliest years of the Republic. At the other extreme, if tribes derive their power through federal delegation, they cannot be given power by Congress that Congress itself does not enjoy. And presumably what Congress gives it can also take away. If it is some combination of the two, as arguably Chief Justice John Marshall suggested in *Cherokee Nation v. Georgia*, 30 U.S. 1 (1831), when he called tribes "domestic dependent nations," the legal issues become exponentially more complex and filled with potential land mines.

Throughout most of American history, observers assumed that tribes would decline in significance. At certain points in history, federal policy was to encourage that decline by encouraging assimilation. At other points, federal policy was to resist that decline by protecting the tribal way of life. But in both cases, observers expected the decline would nevertheless continue. As a result, little attention was accorded to the development of a coherent framework for Indian law.

Recently, however, some tribes have been experiencing an economic boom, driven in part by casino gambling and in part by other factors. To be sure, not all tribes and not all tribal members have benefited from that boom. But it has nevertheless ensured that more attention will be focused on clarifying and systematizing the basic issues of Indian law in the near future.

But it has not happened yet. Recently, in the case of *United States v. Lara*, 541 U.S. 193, 214 (2004), Justice Clarence Thomas called upon the Court "to re-examine the premises and logic of our tribal sovereignty cases" and suggested that much of the "confusion" in Indian law arises from "largely incompatible and doubtful assumptions" underlying the case law. Indeed, the *Lara* case itself is an example of the doctrinal disarray in Indian law. The case—which holds that double jeopardy considerations do not prohibit the federal government from re-prosecuting an offender who has already been prosecuted in tribal court—generated no fewer than six separate opinions. Only a bare majority of five could be garnered for the Court's opinion. (Note that one of the implications of *Lara* is that a tribal government can re-prosecute an alleged offender who has actually been acquitted in federal court and vice versa.)

The proposed Native Hawaiian Government Reorganization Act rides into this morass at full tilt. Because it would authorize the creation (or "reorganization") of what would be by far the largest tribe in history, it puts further pressure on an area of the law that already is showing signs of significant stress. And it raises all sorts of thorny problems. For example, can Congress authorize the Department of Interior to take steps leading to the creation (or even the "reorganization") of a new tribe? Or is it limited to recognizing those groups that are functioning as an independent social and political unit already and have been continuously doing so for a significant period of time?

It is worth pointing out that the Constitution contains no clear statement of Congressional authority to regulate *existing* Indian tribes (as opposed to commerce between the United States and Indian tribes), much less to create or organize additional ones. The authority to regulate existing tribes is sometimes said to derive from the necessity of dealing with reality. The existence of Indian tribes in 1787 (as well as today) is a fact. Surely it was the intention of the Framers to confer power on Congress to deal with that reality, whether it's considered a happy reality, an unhappy reality, or something in between–or so the argument runs.

But the power to authorize the creation of new tribes (or even authorize the reorganization of a previously existing tribe) is not merely the practical power to cope with the world as it is. New tribes and newly reconstituted tribes alter the status quo in significant ways. If the power to create them exists, what limits are placed on it? Does Congress have the authority to create an Indian tribe for Mexican Americans in Southern California? The Amish of Pennsylvania? Orthodox Jews in New York? (Religious groups would be among the groups most likely to desire tribal status, since tribes, if they are conceptualized as sovereign or quasi-sovereign entities are not governed by the Bills of Rights, except insofar as the Indian Civil Rights Act imposes that legal responsibility on the tribe. A religious group could thus arguably surmount the Establishment Clause difficulties dealt with by the Supreme Court in *Board of Education of Kiryas Joel School District v. Grumit*, 512 U.S. 687 (1994), by becoming an tribe).

In examining the constitutionality of the proposed Native Hawaiian Government Reorganization Act, however, we can put all this aside, at least temporarily, because another issue looms much larger. In an age in which racial entitlements are an important feature of the political landscape in nearly every part of the country, the State of Hawaii is in a league by itself. Its Office of Hawaiian Affairs administers a huge public trust—worth billions—that in theory benefits all Hawaiians, but for reasons that are both historical and political, in practice, provides benefits exclusively for ethnic Hawaiians. Among other things, ethnic Hawaiians are eligible for special home loans, business loans, housing and educational programs. On the OHA web site, the caption proudly proclaims its racial loyalty, "Office of Hawaiian Affairs: For the Betterment of Native Hawaiians." The proposed Native Hawaiian Government Reorganization Act is in large measure an effort to preserve this system.

The constitutionality of the system has recently been called into question as a result of the Supreme Court's decision in *Rice v. Cayetano,* 528 U.S. 495 (2000), and the Ninth Circuit's decision in *Doe v. Kamehameha Schools*, 416 F.3d 1025 (9th Cir. 2005). *Rice* held that Hawaii's election system under which only ethnic Hawaiians could vote for Trustees of the Office of Hawaiian Affairs was a violation of the Constitution's Fifteenth Amendment, which prohibits discrimination on the basis of race in voting rights. *Doe* held that the prestigious King Kamehameha schools, which are privately run, cannot give ethnic Hawaiians priority over students of all other races and ethnicities for admission without violating 42 U.S.C. § 1981. Given the results in these cases, it is considered by many to be only a matter of time before other aspects of the OHA's special benefits program will be challenged in court on equal protection and other civil rights grounds and ultimately found contrary to law.

The best hope of those who favor these programs is to transform them from programs that favor one race or ethnicity over others to programs that favor the members of a tribe over non-members. As the Supreme Court held in *Morton v. Mancari*, 417 U.S. 535 (1974), a case involving a hiring preference for tribal members at the U.S. Bureau of Indian Affairs, such a benefit is "granted to Indians not as a discrete racial group, but, rather, as members of quasi-sovereign tribal entities." In other words, it is not race discrimination; it is discrimination on the basis of tribal membership.

The question then boils down to this: Can the United States government and the State of Hawaii achieve by indirection what they very likely could not have achieved directly on account of the Due Process Clause of the Fifth Amendment and the Equal Protection Clause of the Fourteenth Amendment? I would respectfully submit that the answer is no. That is not because *Morton v. Mancari* is not good law. It is. (Note, however, that the *Mancari* decision is a double-edged sword. If discrimination by the Bureau of Indian Affairs *in favor* of tribal members is not race discrimination then presumably discrimination *against* tribal members by a state government is not race discrimination). But it cannot apply to a tribal group that does not yet exist. The very act of transforming ethnic Hawaiians into a tribe is an act performed on a racial group, not a tribal group. When, as here, it is done for the purpose of conferring massive benefits on that group, it is an act of race discrimination subject to strict scrutiny—scrutiny that it likely cannot survive.

The proof of all this is apparent if one simply alters the facts slightly. If the State of Hawaii were operating its special benefits programs for Whites only or for Asians only, no one would dream that the United States could assist them in this scheme by providing a procedure under which Whites or Asians could be declared a tribe.

Testimony on the Native Hawaiian Government Reorganization Act before the U.S. Commission on Civil Rights
Prepared and submitted by Patricia M. Zell in her capacity as former Staff Director and Chief Counsel of the Senate Committee on Indian Affairs
Oral testimony delivered by Noe Kalipi

Overview

There is a history, a course of dealings, and a body of law which inform the special status of the indigenous, native people of the United States. It is a history that begins well before the first European set foot on American shores—it is a history of those who occupied and possessed the lands that were later to become the United States—the aboriginal, indigenous native people of this land who were America's first inhabitants.

The indigenous people did not share similar customs or traditions. Their cultures were diverse. Some of them lived near the ocean and depended upon its bounty for their sustenance. Others made their homes amongst the rocky ledges of mountains and canyons. Some native people fished the rivers, while others gathered berries and roots from the woodlands, harvested rice in the lake areas, and hunted wildlife on the open plains. Their subsistence lifestyles caused some to follow nomadic ways, while others established communities that are well over a thousand years old. Those who later came to America call them "aborigines" or "Indians" or "natives" but the terms were synonymous. Over time, these terms have been used interchangeably to refer to those who occupied and possessed the lands of America prior to European contact.

Although the differences in their languages, their cultures, their belief systems, their customs and traditions, and their geographical origins may have kept them apart and prevented them from developing a shared identity as the native people of this land—with the arrival of western "discoverers" in the United States—their histories are sadly similar. Over time, they were dispossessed of their homelands, removed, relocated, and thousands, if not millions, succumbed to diseases for which they had no immunities and fell victim to the efforts to exterminate them. In the early days of America's history, the native peoples' inherent sovereignty informed the course of the newcomers' dealings with them. Spanish law of the 1500s and 1600s presaged how the United States would recognize their aboriginal title to land, and treaties became the instruments of fostering peaceful relations.[1]

As America's boundaries expanded, new territories came under the protection of the United States. Eventually, as new States entered the Union, there were other aboriginal, indigenous, native people who became recognized as the "aborigines" or "Indians" or "natives" of contemporary times—these included the Eskimos, and the Aleuts, and other native people of Alaska, and later, the indigenous, native people of Hawai'i.

---

[1] Felix S. Cohen, *The Spanish Origin of Indian Rights in the Law of the United States*, 31, GEO. L.J. 1 (1942).

For nearly a century, Federal law has recognized these three groups—American Indians, Alaska Natives, and Native Hawaiians—as comprising the class of people known as Native Americans. Well before the Fourteenth and Fifteenth Amendments to the U.S. Constitution were adopted to address the effects of historic patterns of racial discrimination, the Supreme Court had recognized the unique status of America's native peoples under the Constitution and laws of the United States.

The Native Hawaiian Government Reorganization Act - S. 147

The purpose of S. 147 is to authorize a process for the reorganization of the Native Hawaiian government, to reaffirm the special political and legal relationship between the United States and the Native Hawaiian governing entity, and to provide for the recognition of the Native Hawaiian government by the United States for purposes of carrying on a government-to-government relationship.

Historical Background

On January 17, 1893, the government of the Kingdom of Hawai'i was overthrown by a group of American citizens and others, who acted with the support of U.S. Minister John Stephens and a contingent of U.S. Marines from the U.S.S. Boston. One hundred years later, a resolution extending an apology on behalf of the United States to Native Hawaiians for the illegal overthrow of the Native Hawaiian government and calling for a reconciliation of the relationship between the United States and Native Hawaiians was enacted into law (Public Law 103-150, Apology Resolution). The Apology Resolution acknowledges that the overthrow of the Kingdom of Hawai'i occurred with the active participation of agents and citizens of the United States and further acknowledges that the Native Hawaiian people never directly relinquished their claims to their inherent sovereignty as a people over their national lands to the United States, either through their government or through a plebiscite or referendum.

In December of 1999, the Departments of Interior and Justice initiated a process of reconciliation in response to the Apology Resolution by conducting meetings in Native Hawaiian communities on each of the principal islands in the State of Hawai'i and culminating in two days of open dialogue. In each setting, members of the Native Hawaiian community identified what they believe are the necessary elements of a process to provide for the reconciliation of the relationship between the United States and the Native Hawaiian people. A report, entitled *From Mauka to Makai: The River of Justice Must Flow Freely* (Reconciliation Report), was issued by the two departments on October 23, 2000. The principal recommendation contained in the Reconciliation Report is set forth below:

> Recommendation 1. It is evident from the documentation, statements, and views received during the reconciliation process undertaken by Interior and Justice pursuant to Public Law 103-150 (1993), that the Native Hawaiian people continue to maintain a distinct community and certain governmental structures and they desire to increase their control over their own affairs and institutions. As a matter of justice and equity, this report recommends that the Native Hawaiian people should have self-determination over

their own affairs within the framework of Federal law, as do Native American tribes. For generations, the United States has recognized the rights and promoted the welfare of Native Hawaiians as an indigenous people within our Nation through legislation, administrative action, and policy statements. To safeguard and enhance Native Hawaiian self-determination over their lands, cultural resources, and internal affairs, the Departments believe Congress should enact further legislation to clarify Native Hawaiians' political status and to create a framework for recognizing a government-to-government relationship with a representative Native Hawaiian governing body.[2]

The Constitution of the United States addresses the status of the indigenous, native people of America. That status is founded not upon considerations of race or ethnicity, but upon the historical fact that the indigenous, native people occupied and exercised sovereignty over the lands and territories which were later to become part of the United States. Their sovereignty existed before the formation of the United States, and the United States Constitution recognizes their status as sovereigns, in the same clause of the Constitution that recognizes the sovereignty of the several States and the foreign nations.

The laws of the United States reflect the constitutional status of the indigenous, native people of America. Upon this constitutional foundation, hundreds of Federal laws have been enacted that express the nature of the political and legal relationship the United States has with the sovereign governments of the native people of this land—American Indians, Alaska Natives and Native Hawaiians.

Throughout America's history as a nation, the Executive and Legislative branches of the United States government have entered into treaties and carried on a course of dealings with the indigenous, native people of America, and the Judicial branch of the Federal government has consistently reaffirmed that the treaties and conduct of relations with the indigenous, native people is based on a political and legal relationship.

The U.S. Constitution establishes a legal framework under which the national government has the principal responsibility of conducting relations with America's Native people. As it relates to the Native people of Hawaii, the United States has required in the Hawaii Admissions Act[3] not only that the State of Hawaii must assume a trust responsibility for approximately 203,500 acres of land that had previously been set aside under Federal law in 1921 for Native Hawaiians in the Hawaiian Homes Commission Act,[4] but has further directed that revenues from lands ceded back to the State are to be used for five purposes, one of which is the betterment of the conditions of native Hawaiians. In addition, at the insistence of the United States, the Hawaii State Constitution explicitly recognizes the rights of Native Hawaiians to self-determination and self-governance.

---

[2] U.S. Department of Justice & U.S. Department of the Interior, *From Mauka to Makai: The River of Justice Must Flow Freely*, Report on the Reconciliation Process Between the Federal Government and Native Hawaiians (October 23, 2000), at 17.
[3] Pub. L. No. 83-3, § 5, 73 Stat. 4, 5 (March 18, 1959).
[4] 42 Stat. 108 (July 9, 1921), as amended (Hawaiian Homes Commission Act).

The Congress Has the Constitutional Power and Authority to Address the Conditions of the Indigenous, Native People of America

Although those who first immigrated to America's shores called the indigenous, native people they found here—"Indians"—the terms "Indians" and "Indios" were, for centuries, employed around the world to describe the indigenous, native people of other countries as well. Upon his arrival in Hawaii in 1778, Captain James Cook recorded in his diaries his discovery of the original inhabitants of Hawaii, referring to the native people as "Indians". In a similar manner, the term "tribe" was the word Europeans assigned to the sovereign nations or groups of America's indigenous, native people.

While the U.S. Constitution vests the Congress with authority to conduct relations with Indian tribes, the U.S. Supreme Court has upheld the Congress' exercise of its constitutional authority as applied to the indigenous, native people of Alaska – not all of whom are organized as Indian tribes. And since 1910, Congress has enacted over 160 Federal laws that address the conditions of the indigenous, native people of Hawaii.

The indigenous, native people of America are not all "Indians" nor are they all organized as "tribes", but they do share the same status under the U.S. Constitution and Federal law—a status which arises out of their inherent sovereignty and the fact that their sovereignty pre-existed the formation of the United States.

As early as the 1830's, U.S. Supreme Court Chief Justice John Marshall articulated these principles in the Court's rulings, and from that time forward, the Supreme Court has continued to sustain the constitutionality of Federal laws that are built upon the legal foundation of the political and legal relationships that the United States has had for more than two hundred years with the indigenous, native people who exercised sovereignty in America prior to the establishment of the United States—American Indians, Alaska Natives, and Native Hawaiians.

In contemporary times, it is the U.S. Supreme Court's rulings that have expressly held that those laws are not based on race or ethnicity, and that Congress has the authority to address the conditions of the indigenous, native people of the United States.[5]

In 1934, with the enactment of the Indian Reorganization Act, the Congress provided a process for the reorganization of tribal governments in Indian country—governments that had been discouraged by U.S. policies and laws from exercising their inherent sovereignty. The U.S. Supreme Court has repeatedly sustained Congress' exercise of its constitutional authority in enacting the Indian Reorganization Act.

S. 147 provides a process for the reorganization of a Native Hawaiian government so that the indigenous, native people of Hawaii might give expression to their rights as one group of

---

[5] *Morton v. Mancari*, 417 U.S. 535 (1974).

America's native people to self-determination and self-governance, consistent with the United States' policy of the past 36 years.

Public Briefing on the Akaka Bill
H. William Burgess[6]

For the last eight years, my wife and I have been advocating and litigating pro bono to bring to life in Hawaii the first of America's self evident truths: That all men are created equal; i.e., that every person, whatever his or her ancestry, is entitled to the equal protection of the laws.

Since the summer of 2000, she and I, as part of our quest for equality for all, have been actively lobbying against the Akaka bill.

Hawaiian entitlements and the Akaka bill have also had the attention of the Commission on Civil Rights for some time. In September 2000, the Commission sent several of its Commissioners and staff to Honolulu for a two-day forum devoted to the theory that *Rice v. Cayetano* (handed down by the United States Supreme Court on February 23, 2000) violated the civil rights of native Hawaiians and the way to overcome that was to pass the Akaka bill.

That forum with the Hawaii Advisory Committee of the U.S. Commission on Civil Rights was entitled "The Impact of the Decision in *Rice v. Cayetano* on Entitlements." I testified at that hearing along with the late brilliant attorney, Patrick Hanifin, and Ken Conklin. But despite our testimony, the lengthy report published after that forum concluded and recommended that respect for the civil rights of Native Hawaiians required that they should have the option of seceding from the United States and becoming an independent nation.

Now, over five years later, that far-out recommendation has not been followed; but the Akaka bill is still pending and it is still supported by powerful well-funded interests and it hangs like a cloud over the Aloha State. The many people in Hawaii who oppose the bill[7] are glad that the United States Commission on Civil Rights is now revisiting this important question. I urge you to now adhere to America's highest ideals and recommend that Hawaii be preserved as one state undivided with equality and Aloha for all.

Background of the Akaka Bill

The original version of S. 147, commonly referred to as the "Akaka bill," was first introduced in the year 2000 shortly after the Supreme Court, in *Rice v. Cayetano,* struck down the racial restriction on voting for the Office of Hawaiian Affairs. Because that decision threatened many other laws and programs for the "benefit" of Hawaiians, Senator Akaka with Senator Inouye's endorsement, proposed candidly to circumvent the Supreme Court's decision by having Congress "recognize" Hawaiians (defined substantially the same way the Supreme Court had held in *Rice* to be "racial") as the equivalent of an Indian tribe.

---

6 Aloha for All, is a multi-ethnic group of men and women, all residents, taxpayers and property owners in Hawaii. We believe that Aloha is for everyone; every citizen is entitled to the equal protection of the laws without regard to her or his ancestry. For further information about the Akaka bill see: http://www.aloha4all.org (click on Q&A's) and http://www.angelfire.com/hi2/hawaiiansovereignty/OpposeAkakaBill.html or email hwburgess@hawaii.rr.com.
7. Hawaii residents oppose the bill by a margin of 2 to 1. The comprehensive statewide telephone survey completed July 10, 2005 shows 67% responding to the question are against the Akaka bill.

The bill encountered resistance and did not pass in 2000 or subsequently. (It did pass a sparsely attended House in 2000 when Representative Abercrombie included it in a vote on non-controversial items.) Efforts to attach it as a rider to appropriations bills in 2000, 2001 and 2004 were defeated. Hawaii's political leaders have resubmitted the bill to the 109th Congress as S. 147 and H.R. 309. It was expected to reach the Senate floor before August 7, 2005, but that was postponed because of Hurricane Katrina and the replacement of Supreme Court Justice Rehnquist and later, Justice Sandra Day O'Connor.

A Radical Change in Existing Law

Although the proponents assert the bill will simply give Native Hawaiians "parity" with the Federal Government's treatment of American Indians and Alaska Natives, that is not true. The bill would in reality make a radical change in existing law. The bill would give Native Hawaiians, merely because of their ancestry, something no American Indian has: the right to create the equivalent of a tribe where none now exists.

For Native Americans, ancestry alone confers no special status. Membership in a tribe that has existed continuously is required. According to Census 2000, there are over 4 million people with some Native American ancestry. But less than 2 million of them are members of recognized tribes and only those recognized tribes can have a government-to-government relationship with the United States.

Congress may "acknowledge" or "recognize" groups which have existed as tribes, i.e., autonomous quasi-sovereign governing entities, continuously from historic times to the present, *see* 25 C.F.R. § 83.7, but it has no power to create a tribe arbitrarily, *see United States v. Sandoval*, 231 U.S. 28 (1913). An attorney from the Department of Justice has put it succinctly, "We don't create tribes out of thin air."[8]

In 1790 (20 years before 1810 when he unified the Hawaiian islands), Kamehameha the Great brought John Young and Isaac Davis on to join his forces and welcomed them into his family. Non-natives thereafter continued to intermarry, assimilate and contribute to the governance under the great King and under every subsequent government of Hawaii since then, both in high governmental positions as cabinet members, judges, elected legislators, and as ordinary citizens.

Unlike the history of Native Americans, there has never been in Hawaii, even during the years of the Kingdom, any "tribe" or government of any kind for Native Hawaiians separate from the government of the rest of Hawaii's citizens. The Hawaiians-only nation the Akaka bill proposes to "reorganize" has never existed. *See* Patrick W. Hanifin, *To Dwell on the Earth in Unity: Rice, Arakaki, and the Growth of Citizenship and Voting Rights in Hawaii, at*

---

8 *See generally Connecticut ex rel. Blumenthal v. United States Department of the Interior*, 228 F.3d 82 (2nd Cir. 2000). Alice Thurston argued on behalf of the Secretary of the Interior, "When the Department of Interior recognizes tribes, it is not saying, 'You are a tribe.' It is saying, 'We recognize that your sovereignty exists.' We don't create tribes out of thin air." JEFF BENEDICT, WITHOUT RESERVATION: HOW A CONTROVERSIAL INDIAN TRIBE ROSE TO POWER AND BUILT THE WORLD'S LARGEST CASINO 352 (2001).

http://www.angelfire.com/hi2/hawaiiansovereignty/HanifinCitizen.pdf (last visited Mar. 15, 2006).

Our friends, neighbors, fellow professionals, judges, political leaders. aunties, uncles, nieces, nephews, calabash cousins, spouses and loved ones of Hawaiian ancestry are governed by the same federal, state and local governments as the rest of us. That is why Congress cannot use laws applicable to Indian tribes to create a new government in Hawaii.

Senator Inouye, in his remarks on introduction of S. 147/H.R.309, *see* 151 CONG. REC. S450 (daily ed., Jan. 25, 2005), concedes that federal Indian law does not provide the authority for Congress to create a Native Hawaiian governing entity:

> Because the Native Hawaiian government is not an Indian tribe, the body of Federal Indian law that would otherwise customarily apply when the United States extends Federal recognition to an Indian tribal group does not apply.

> That is why concerns which are premised on the manner in which Federal Indian law provides for the respective governmental authorities of the state governments and Indian tribal governments simply don't apply in Hawaii.

There Being No Tribe, the Constitution Applies

The Akaka bill stumbles over the Constitution with virtually every step it takes.

- As soon as the bill is enacted, superior political rights are granted to Native Hawaiians, defined by ancestry in S. 147 §7(a). The U.S. is deemed to have recognized the right of Native Hawaiians to form their own new government and to adopt its organic governing documents. No one else in the United States has that right. This creates a hereditary aristocracy in violation of Article I, Sec. 9, U.S. Const. "No Title of Nobility shall be granted by the United States."

- Also, under S. 147 §8(a), upon enactment, the delegation by the United States of authority to the State of Hawaii to "address the conditions of the indigenous, native people of Hawaii" in the Admission Act "is reaffirmed." This delegation to the State of authority to single out one ancestral group for special privilege would also seem to violate the prohibition against hereditary aristocracy. The Constitution forbids the United States from granting titles of nobility itself and also precludes the United States from authorizing states to bestow hereditary privilege.

- S. 147 §7(b)(2)(A) & (B) would require the Secretary of the Interior to appoint a commission of nine members who "shall be Native Hawaiian." Restricting federal appointments based on race would violate the Equal Protection Clause of the Fifth Amendment, among other laws, and would require the Secretary to violate her oath to uphold the Constitution.

26

- Section 7(c) of the proposed legislation would require the Commission to prepare a roll of adult Native Hawaiians and the Secretary to publish the racially restricted roll in the Federal Register and thereafter update it. Same Constitutional violations as immediately above.

- Under Section 7(c)(2) of the proposed legislation, persons on the roll may develop the criteria and structure of an Interim Governing Council and elect members from the roll to that Council. Racial restrictions on electors and upon candidates both violate the Fifteenth Amendment and the Voting Rights Act.

- Under Section 7(c)(2)(B)(iii)(I) of the proposed legislation, the Council may conduct a referendum among those on the roll to determine the proposed elements of the organic governing documents of the Native Hawaiian governing entity. Racial restrictions on persons allowed to vote in the referendum would violate the Fifteenth Amendment and the Voting Rights Act.

- Under Section 7(c)(2)(B)(iii)(IV) of the proposed legislation, the Council, based on the referendum, may develop proposed organic documents and hold elections by persons on the roll to ratify them. This would be the third racially restricted election and third violation of the Fiftteenth Amendment and the Voting Rights Act.

- Section 7(c)(4)(A) would require the Secretary to certify that the organic governing documents comply with seven listed requirements. Use of the roll to make the certification would violate the Equal Protection Clause of the Fifth Amendment, among other laws, and would, again, require the Secretary to violate her oath to uphold the Constitution.

- Under Section 7(c)(5) of the proposed legislation, once the Secretary issues the certification, the Council may hold elections of the officers of the new government. If these elections restrict the right to vote based on race, as seems very likely, they would violate the Fifteenth Amendment and the Voting Rights Act.

- Under Section 7(c) of the proposed legislation, upon the election of the officers, the United States, without any further action of Congress or the Executive Branch, would "reaffirm the political and legal relationship between the U.S. and the Native Hawaiian governing entity" and would recognize the Native Hawaiian governing body as the "representative governing body of the Native Hawaiian people." This would violate the Equal Protection clause of the Fifth and Fourteenth Amendments by giving one racial group political power and status and their own sovereign government. These special relationships with the United States are denied to any other citizens.

- Under Section 8(b) of the proposed legislation, the three governments would then be permitted to then negotiate an agreement for the transfer of lands, natural resources and other assets; the delegation of governmental power and authority to the new government; the exercise of civil and criminal jurisdiction by the new government; and the "residual responsibilities" of the United States and the State of Hawaii to the new government.

This *carte blanche* grant of authority to officials of the State and Federal governments to agree to give away public lands, natural resources and other assets to the new government, without receiving anything in return, is beyond all existing constitutional limitations on the power of the Federal and State of Hawaii executive branches. Even more extreme is the authority to surrender the sovereignty and jurisdiction of the State of Hawaii over some or all of the lands and surrounding waters of some or all of the islands of the State of Hawaii and over some or all of the people of Hawaii. Likewise, the general power to commit the Federal and State governments to "residual responsibilities" to the new Native Hawaiian government.

- Under Section 8(b)(2) of the proposed legislation, the three governments would be permitted to, but would not be required to, submit to Congress and to the Governor and legislature of the State of Hawaii amendments to federal and state laws that will enable implementation of the agreement. Treaties with foreign governments require the approval of two-thirds of the Senate. Constitutional amendments require the consent of the citizens. But the Akaka bill does not require the consent of the citizens of Hawaii or of Congress or of the State of Hawaii legislature to the terms of the agreement. Under the bill, the only mention is that the parties may recommend amendments to implement the terms to which they have agreed.

  Given the dynamics at the bargaining table created by the bill—where the State officials are driven by the same urge they now exhibit, to curry favor with what they view as the "swing" vote; where Federal officials are perhaps constrained with a similar inclination; and where the new Native Hawaiian government officials have the duty to their constituents to demand the maximum—it is not likely that the agreement reached will be moderate or that any review by Congress or the Hawaii legislature will be sought if it can be avoided. More likely is that the State will proceed under the authority of the Akaka bill to promptly implement whatever deal has been made.

The Myth of Past Injustices and Economic Deprivations

Contrary to the claims of the bill supporters, the United States took no lands from Hawaiians at the time of the 1893 revolution or the 1898 Annexation (or at any other time), and it did not deprive them of sovereignty. As part of the Annexation Act, the United States provided compensation by assuming the debts of about $4 million which had been incurred by the Kingdom. The lands ceded to the Untied States were government lands under the Kingdom held for the benefit of all citizens without regard to race. They still are. Private land titles were unaffected by the overthrow or annexation. Upon annexation, ordinary Hawaiians became full citizens of the United States with more freedom, security, opportunity for prosperity and sovereignty than they ever had under the Kingdom.

Nor do Native Hawaiians suffer from the grinding poverty of Native American tribes. The Senate Indian Affairs Committee notes that "the vast majority of Native economies are moribund" "with unemployment averaging 45 percent" and that "per capita income for Indians averages $8,284." *See* Committee on Indian Affairs, United States Senate, *Views and Estimates of the FY 2005 Budget Request* 3-4 (Mar. 3, 2004), *at* http://www.nihb.org/docs/fy05_scia_views.pdf (last visited Mar. 15, 2006).

By contrast, Census 2000 shows per capita income for Native Hawaiians in Hawaii at $14,199 and median family income of $49,282. For the 60,000 Native Hawaiians residing in California, where they are free from the incentive-smothering entitlement programs provided in Hawaii, the per capita income of Native Hawaiians is $19,881 and median family income is $55,770. Striking evidence that Native Hawaiians are fully capable of prospering, without being wards of the Department of the Interior and without entitlements from the State of Hawaii, is shown in the Census 2000 reports of median per capita income of male, full time, year-round Native Hawaiian workers: $33,258 in Hawaii and $38,997 in California.

Hawaiians today are no different, in any constitutionally significant way, from any other ethnic group in Hawaii's multi-ethnic, intermarried, integrated society. Like all the rest of us, some do well, some do not and most are somewhere in between.

Rejection of Democracy and Aloha

Today the State of Hawaii is, by law as well as by aspiration, a multiracial, thoroughly integrated state. The Akaka bill is a frontal assault on both Aloha and the American ideal of equality under the law. It would elevate one racial group to the status of a hereditary elite to be supported by citizens who are not of the favored race. As United States District Judge Helen Gillmor said in *Arakaki I*, "This Court is mindful that ours is a political system that strives to govern its citizens as individuals rather than as groups. The Supreme Court's brightest moments have affirmed this idea (citing *Brown v. Board of Education* and other cases), while its darkest moments have rejected this concept (citing *Dred Scott*, *Plessy v. Ferguson*, *Bradwell v. Illinois* and *Korematsu*)." *Arakaki v. Hawaii*, 2000 U.S. Dist. LEXIS 22394, *3-4 (D. Hi. 2000).

For a comprehensive section-by-section analysis of the bill, please see Paul Sullivan, *Killing Aloha: The Native Hawaiian Recognition Bill is Wrong for Native Hawaiians, Wrong for the State of Hawaii, and Wrong for the United States*, *at* http://www.angelfire.com/hi5/bigfiles2/AkakaSullivan012505.pdf (last visited Mar. 15, 2006).

Keep Hawaii One State Indivisible

Carving up Hawaii into separate sovereign enclaves would hurt all of us, whether we are of Hawaiian or any other ancestry. A house divided against itself cannot stand. The Constitution "looks to an indestructible union, composed of indestructible States." *Texas v. White*, 7 Wallace 700 (1869).

The Authority of Congress to Establish a Process for Recognizing a Reconstituted Native Hawaiian Governing Entity
Viet D. Dinh
H. Christopher Bartolomucci

This chapter addresses Congress' authority to enact S. 147, the proposed Native Hawaiian Government Reorganization Act of 2005 ("NHGRA"), which establishes a process for reconstituting and recognizing the Native Hawaiian governing entity. We conclude that Congress has the constitutional authority to enact the Native Hawaiian Government Reorganization Act of 2005.

Congress possesses plenary and exclusive power under the Constitution to enact special legislation to deal with Native Americans. This authority, inherent in the Constitution and explicit in the Indian Commerce Clause, art. I, § 8, cl. 3, and Treaty Clause, art. II, § 2, cl. 2, extends to dealings with Native Hawaiians, especially given the particular moral and legal obligations the United States assumed for its role in effecting a forcible end to the Kingdom of Hawaii in 1893.

Rice v. Cayetano, 528 U.S. 495 (2000), is not to the contrary. The Supreme Court there expressly declined to address whether "native Hawaiians have a status like that of Indians in organized tribes" and "whether Congress may treat the native Hawaiians as it does the Indian tribes." *Id.* at 518. The conclusion that granting Native Hawaiians special voting rights in connection with the election of a state governmental official violates the Equal Protection Clause does not speak to whether Congress has the authority to reaffirm the status of Native Hawaiians as an indigenous, self-governing people and reestablish a government-to-government relationship:

> The decisions of this Court leave no doubt that federal legislation with respect to Indian tribes, although relating to Indians as such, is not based upon impermissible racial classifications. Quite the contrary, classifications expressly singling out Indian tribes as subjects of legislation are expressly provided for in the Constitution and supported by the ensuing history of the Federal Government's relations with Indians.

United States v. Antelope, 430 U.S. 641, 645 (1977).

I. The Native Hawaiian Government Reorganization Act

The stated purpose of the NHGRA is "to provide a process for the reorganization of the Native Hawaiian governing entity and the reaffirmation of the political and legal relationship between the United States and the Native Hawaiian governing entity for purposes of continuing a government-to-government relationship." NHGRA § 4(b). To that end, the NHGRA authorizes the Secretary of the Interior to establish a Commission that will prepare and maintain a roll of Native Hawaiians wishing to participate in the reorganization of the Native Hawaiian governing entity. *Id.* § 7(b). For the purpose of establishing the roll, the NHGRA defines the term "Native Hawaiian" as:

> (A) an individual who is one of the indigenous, native people of Hawaii and who is a direct lineal descendant of the aboriginal, indigenous, native people who (i) resided in the islands that now comprise the State of Hawaii on or before January 1, 1893; and (ii) occupied and exercised sovereignty in the Hawaiian archipelago, including the area that now constitutes the State of Hawaii; or (B) an individual who is one of the indigenous, native people of Hawaii and who was eligible in 1921 for the programs authorized by the Hawaiian Homes Commission Act (42 Stat. 108, chapter 42) or a direct lineal descendant of that individual.

Id. § 3(8).

Through the preparation and maintenance of the roll of Native Hawaiians, the Commission will set up a Native Hawaiian Interim Governing Council called for by the NHGRA. *Id.* § 7(c)(2). Native Hawaiians listed on the roll may develop criteria for candidates to be elected to serve on the Council; determine the Council's structure; and elect members of the Council from enrolled Native Hawaiians. *Id.* § 7(c)(2)(A).

The NHGRA provides that the Council may conduct a referendum among enrolled Native Hawaiians "for the purpose of determining the proposed elements of the organic governing documents of the Native Hawaiian governing entity." *Id.* § 7(c)(2)(B)(iii)(I). Thereafter, the Council may hold elections for the purpose of ratifying the proposed organic governing documents and electing the officers of the Native Hawaiian governing entity. *Id.* § 7(c)(2)(B)(iii)(IV).

II. Congress' Authority to Enact the NHGRA

Congressional authority to enact S. 147 encompasses two subordinate questions: First, would Congress have the power to adopt such legislation for members of a Native American tribe in the contiguous 48 states? Second, does such power extend to Native Hawaiians? The answer to both questions is yes, especially given the moral and legal obligations the United States acquired for overthrowing the then-sovereign Kingdom of Hawaii in 1893.

A. Congress' Broad Power to Deal with Indians Includes the Power to Restore Sovereignty to, and Reorganize the Government of, Indian Tribes

There is little question that Congress has the power to recognize Indian tribes. As the Supreme Court explained recently, "the Constitution grants Congress broad general powers to legislate in respect to Indian tribes, powers that we have consistently described as 'plenary and exclusive.' " *United States v. Lara*, 541 U.S. 193, 200 (2004). *See also South Dakota v. Yankton Sioux Tribe*, 522 U.S. 329, 343 (1998) ("Congress possesses plenary power over Indian affairs"); *Alaska v. Native Village of Venetie Tribal Gov't*, 522 U.S. 520, 531 n.6 (1998) (same); 20 U.S.C. § 4101(3) (finding that the Constitution "invests the Congress with plenary power over the field of Indian affairs"). The NHGRA expressly recites and invokes this constitutional authority. See NHGRA § 2(1) ("The Constitution vests Congress with the authority to address the conditions of the indigenous native people of the United States."); *id.* § 4(a)(3).

This broad congressional power derives from a number of constitutional provisions, including the Indian Commerce Clause, art. I, § 8, cl. 3, which grants Congress the power to "regulate Commerce * * * with the Indian Tribes," as well as the Treaty Clause, art. II, § 2, cl. 2. *See Lara*, 541 U.S. at 200-01; *Morton v. Mancari*, 417 U.S. 535, 552 (1974). Other sources of constitutional authority include the Debt Clause, art. I, § 8, cl. 1, *see United States v. Sioux Nation of Indians*, 448 U.S. 371, 397 (1980); see *also Pope v. United States*, 323 U.S. 1, 9 (1944) ("The power of Congress to provide for the payment of debts, conferred by § 8 of Article I of the Constitution, is not restricted to payment of those obligations which are legally binding on the Government. It extends to the creation of such obligations in recognition of claims which are merely moral or honorary."); and the Property Clause, art. IV, § 3, cl. 2, *see Alaska Pacific Fisheries v. United States*, 248 U.S. 78, 87-88 (1918); *see also Alabama v. Texas*, 347 U.S. 272, 273 (1954) (per curiam) ("The power of Congress to dispose of any kind of property belonging to the United States is vested in Congress without limitation.") (internal quotation marks omitted).[9]

Congress' legislative authority with respect to Indians also rests in part "upon the Constitution's adoption of preconstitutional powers necessarily inherent in any Federal Government, namely power that this Court has described as 'necessary concomitants of nationality.' " *Lara*, 124 S. Ct. at 1634 (citing, *inter alia, United States v. Curtiss-Wright Export Corp.*, 299 U.S. 304, 315-322 (1936)). *See also Morton v. Mancari*, 417 U.S. at 551-552 ("The plenary power of Congress to deal with the special problems of Indians is drawn both explicitly and implicitly from the Constitution itself.") (emphasis added).

Plenary congressional authority to recognize Indian tribes extends to the restoration and reorganization of tribal sovereignty. In *Lara,* the Court held that Congress' broad authority with respect to Indians includes the power to enact legislation designed to "relax restrictions" on "tribal sovereign authority." 124 S. Ct. at 196, 202. "From the Nation's beginning," the Court said, "Congress' need for such legislative power would have seemed obvious." *Id.* at 202. The Court explained that "the Government's Indian policies, applicable to numerous tribes with diverse cultures, affecting billions of acres of land, of necessity would fluctuate dramatically as the needs of the Nation and those of the tribes changed over time," and "[s]uch major policy changes inevitably involve major changes in the metes and bounds of tribal sovereignty." *Id.* The Court noted that today congressional policy "seeks greater tribal autonomy within the framework of a 'government-to-government' relationship with federal agencies." *Id.* (quoting 59 Fed. Reg. 22,951 (1994)).

Of particular significance to the present analysis, the Court in *Lara* specifically recognized Congress' power to restore previously extinguished sovereign relations with Indian

---

9 As discussed herein, *see infra* at 16-17, Congress in 1921 set aside some 200,000 acres of public land for the benefit of Native Hawaiians. The NHGRA is related to, and would help to realize the purpose of, that exercise of the Property Clause power by commencing a process that would result in the identification of the proper beneficiaries of Congress' set aside.

tribes. The Court observed that "Congress has restored previously extinguished tribal status -- by re-recognizing a Tribe whose tribal existence it previously had terminated." *Id.* (citing Congress' restoration of the Menominee tribe in 25 U.S.C. §§ 903-903f). And the Court cited the 1898 annexation of Hawaii as an example of Congress' power "to modify the degree of autonomy enjoyed by a dependent sovereign that is not a State." *Id.* Thus, when it comes to the sovereignty of Indian tribes or other "domestic dependent nations," *Cherokee Nation v. Georgia*, 30 U.S. 1, 17 (1831), the Constitution does not "prohibit Congress from changing the relevant legal circumstances, i.e., from taking actions that modify or adjust the tribes' status," and it is not for the federal judiciary to "second-guess the political branches' own determinations" in that regard. *Lara*, 124 S. Ct. at 205.

United States v. John, 437 U.S. 634 (1978), further supports congressional authority to recognize reconstituted tribal governments and to reestablish sovereign relations with them. There, Congress' power to legislate with respect to the Choctaw Indians of Mississippi was challenged on grounds that "since 1830 the Choctaw residing in Mississippi have become fully assimilated into the political and social life of the State" and that "the Federal Government long ago abandoned its supervisory authority over these Indians." *Id.* at 652. It was thus urged that to "recognize the Choctaws in Mississippi as Indians over whom special federal power may be exercised would be anomalous and arbitrary." *Id.* The Court unanimously rejected the argument. "[W]e do not agree that Congress and the Executive Branch have less power to deal with the affairs of the Mississippi Choctaw than with the affairs of other Indian groups." *Id.* at 652-653. The "fact that federal supervision over them has not been continuous," according to the Court, does not "destroy[…] the federal power to deal with them." *Id.* at 653.

Congress exercised this established authority to restore the government-to-government relationship with the Menominee Indian tribe of Wisconsin, *see Lara*, 541 U.S. at 203-204, and it can do the same here. Indeed, the NHGRA government reorganization process closely resembles that prescribed by the Menominee Restoration Act, 25 U.S.C. §§ 903-903f.

In 1954, Congress adopted the Menominee Indian Termination Act, 25 U.S.C. §§ 891-902, which terminated the government-to-government relationship with the tribe, ended federal supervision over it, closed its membership roll, and provided that "the laws of the several States shall apply to the tribe and its members in the same manner as they apply to other citizens or persons within their jurisdiction." *Menominee Tribe of Indians v. United States*, 391 U.S. 404, 407-410 (1968). In 1973, Congress reversed course and adopted the Menominee Restoration Act, which repealed the Termination Act, restored the sovereign relationship with the tribe, reinstated the tribe's rights and privileges under federal law, and reopened its membership roll. 25 U.S.C. §§ 903a(b), 903b(c).

The Menominee Restoration Act established a process for reconstituting the Menominee tribal leadership and organic documents under the direction of the Secretary of the Interior. The Restoration Act directed the Secretary to: (a) announce the date of a general council meeting of the tribe to nominate candidates for election to a newly-created, nine-member Menominee Restoration Committee; (b) hold an election to elect the members of the Committee; and (c) approve the Committee so elected if the Restoration Act's nomination and election requirements were met. *Id.* § 903b(a). Just so with S. 147. The NHGRA authorizes the Secretary of the

Interior to establish a Commission that will prepare and maintain a roll of Native Hawaiians wishing to participate in the reorganization of the Native Hawaiian governing entity. NHGRA § 7(b). The NHGRA provides for the establishment of a Native Hawaiian Interim Governing Council. *Id.* § 7(c)(2). Native Hawaiians listed on the roll may develop criteria for candidates to be elected to serve on the Council; determine the Council's structure; and elect members of the Council from enrolled Native Hawaiians. *Id.* § 7(c)(2)(A).

The Menominee Restoration Act provided that, following the election of the Menominee Restoration Committee, and at the Committee's request, the Secretary was to conduct an election "for the purpose of determining the tribe's constitution and bylaws." *Id.* § 903c(a). After the adoption of such documents, the Committee was to hold an election "for the purpose of determining the individuals who will serve as tribal officials as provided in the tribal constitution and bylaws." *Id.* § 903c(c). Likewise, the NHGRA provides that the Native Hawaiian Interim Governing Council may conduct a referendum among enrolled Native Hawaiians "for the purpose of determining the proposed elements of the organic governing documents of the Native Hawaiian governing entity." *Id.* § 7(c)(2)(B)(iii)(I). Thereafter, the Council may hold elections for the purpose of ratifying the proposed organic governing documents and electing the officers of the Native Hawaiian governing entity. *Id.* § 7(c)(2)(B)(iii)(IV).

The courts have approved the process set forth in the Menominee Restoration Act to restore sovereignty to the Menominee Indians. *See Lara*, 541 U.S. at 203 (citing the Restoration Act as an example where Congress "restored previously extinguished tribal rights"); *United States v. Long*, 324 F.3d 475, 483 (7th Cir.) (concluding that Congress had the power to "restor[e] to the Menominee the inherent sovereign power that it took from them in 1954"), *cert. denied*, 540 U.S. 822 (2003). The teachings of these cases would apply to validate the similar process set forth in NHGRA.

B. Congress' Power to Enact Special Legislation with Respect to Indians Extends to Native Hawaiians

The inquiry, therefore, turns to whether Congress has the same authority to deal with Native Hawaiians as it does with other Native Americans in the contiguous 48 states. Congress has concluded that it has such authority. *See* NHGRA § 4(a)(3) (finding that Congress "possesses the authority under the Constitution, including but not limited to Article I, section 8, clause 3, to enact legislation to address the conditions of Native Hawaiians"); 42 U.S.C. § 11701(17) ("The authority of the Congress under the United States Constitution to legislate in matters affecting the aboriginal or indigenous peoples of the United States includes the authority to legislate in matters affecting the native peoples of Alaska and Hawaii."). We conclude that courts will likely affirm these assertions of congressional authority.[10]

Under *United States v. Sandoval*, 231 U.S. 28 (1913), Congress has the authority to recognize and deal with native groups pursuant to its Indian affairs power, and courts have only a

---

10 *Rice v. Cayetano* did not decide the issue. On the contrary, the Supreme Court in *Rice* expressly declined to answer the questions whether "native Hawaiians have a status like that of Indians in organized tribes" and "whether Congress may treat the native Hawaiians as it does the Indian tribes." 528 U.S. at 518.

very limited role in reviewing the exercise of such congressional authority. In *Sandoval*, the Supreme Court rejected the argument that Congress lacked authority to treat the Pueblos of New Mexico as Indians and that the Pueblos were "beyond the range of congressional power under the Constitution." *Id*. at 49.

The Court first observed that "[n]ot only does the Constitution expressly authorize Congress to regulate commerce with the Indian tribes, but long continued legislative and executive usage and an unbroken current of judicial decisions have attributed to the United States * * * the power and duty of exercising a fostering care and protection over all dependent Indian communities within its borders, whether within its original territory or territory subsequently acquired, and whether within or without the limits of a state." *Id*. at 45-46. The Court went on to say that, although "it is not meant by this that Congress may bring a community or body of people within the range of this power by arbitrarily calling them an Indian tribe," nevertheless, "the questions whether, to what extent, and for what time they shall be recognized and dealt with as dependent tribes requiring the guardianship and protection of the United States are to be determined by Congress, and not by the courts." *Id*. at 46. Applying those principles, the Supreme Court concluded that Congress' "assertion of guardianship over [the Pueblos] cannot be said to be arbitrary, but must be regarded as both authorized and controlling." *Id*. at 47. And the Court so held even though the Pueblos differed (in the Court's view) in some respects from other Indians: They were not "nomadic in their inclinations"; they were "disposed to peace"; they "liv[ed] in separate and isolated communities"; their lands were "held in communal, fee-simple ownership under grants from the King of Spain"; and they possibly had become citizens of the United States. *Id*. at 39.

Sandoval thus holds, first, that Congress, in exercising its constitutional authority to deal with Indian tribes, may determine whether a "community or body of people" is amenable to that authority, and, second, that unless Congress acts "arbitrarily," courts do not second-guess Congress' determination.[11]

It cannot be said that the NHGRA is an arbitrary exercise of Congress' power to recognize and deal with this Nation's native peoples. Congress has expressly found, in the NHGRA and other statutes, that Native Hawaiians are like other Native Americans. *See* NHGRA § 2(2) (finding that Native Hawaiians "are indigenous, native people of the United States"); *Id*. § 2(20)(B) (Congress "has identified Native Hawaiians as a distinct group of indigenous, native people of the United States within the scope of its authority under the Constitution, and has enacted scores of statutes on their behalf"); *id*. § 4(a)(1); Native American Languages Act, 25 U.S.C. § 2902(1) ("The term 'Native American' means an Indian, Native Hawaiian, or Native American Pacific Islander"); American Indian Religious Freedom Act, 42 U.S.C. § 1996 (declaring it to be the policy of the United States "to protect and preserve for American Indians their inherent right of freedom to believe, express, and exercise the traditional religions of the

---

11 *See also Lara*, 541 U.S. at 205 (federal judiciary should not "second-guess the political branches' own determinations" with respect to "the metes and bounds of tribal autonomy"); *United States v. McGowan*, 302 U.S. 535, 538 (1938) ("Congress alone has the right to determine the manner in which this country's guardianship over the Indians shall be carried out"); *Long*, 324 F.3d at 482 ("[W]hile we assume that Congress neither can nor would confer the status of a tribe onto a random group of people, we have no doubt about congressional power to recognize an ancient group of people for what they are."); *cf. Alaska v. Native Village of Venetie*, 522 U.S. at 534 ("Whether the concept of Indian country should be modified is a question entirely for Congress.").

American Indian, Eskimo, Aleut, and Native Hawaiians"); 42 U.S.C. § 11701(1) (finding that "Native Hawaiians comprise a distinct and unique indigenous people with a historical continuity to the original inhabitants of the Hawaiian archipelago whose society was organized as a Nation prior to the arrival of the first nonindigenous people in 1778").

Congress' authority to treat Native Hawaiians as American Indians is supported by the numerous statutes Congress has enacted doing just that. *See, e.g.,* Hawaiian Homes Commission Act, 42 Stat. 108 (1921); Native Hawaiian Education Act, 20 U.S.C. §§ 7511-7517; Hawaiian Homelands Homeownership Act, 25 U.S.C. §§ 4221-4243; Native Hawaiian Health Care Act, 42 U.S.C. 11701(19) (noting Congress' "enactment of federal laws which extend to the Hawaiian people the same rights and privileges accorded to American Indian, Alaska Native, Eskimo, and Aleut communities"); *see also* Statement of U.S. Representative Ed Case, Hearing Before the Senate Committee on Indian Affairs on S. 147, the Native Hawaiian Government Reorganization Act, at 2-3 (March 1, 2005) ("[O]ver 160 federal statutes have enacted programs to better the conditions of Native Hawaiians in areas such as Hawaiian homelands, health, education and economic development, all exercises of Congress' plenary authority under our U.S. Constitution to address the conditions of indigenous peoples.") (prepared text) (hereinafter, "Senate Indian Affairs Committee Hearing on S. 147"); *cf.* Apology Resolution, Pub. L. No. 103-150, 107 Stat. 1510 (1993). No court has struck down any of these numerous legislative actions as unconstitutional.

That Congress has power to enact special legislation for Native Hawaiians is made clear by congressional action dealing with Native Alaskans, who-- like Native Hawaiians -- differ from American Indian tribes anthropologically, historically, and culturally. In 1971, Congress adopted the Alaska Native Claims Settlement Act ("ANCSA"), 43 U.S.C. §§ 1601-1629h, which is predicated on the view that congressional power to deal with Native Alaskans is coterminous with its plenary authority relating to American Indian tribes. *See* 43 U.S.C. § 1601(a) (finding a need for settlement of all claims "by Natives and Native groups of Alaska"); *id.* § 1602(b) (defining "Native" as a U.S. citizen "who is a person of one-fourth degree of more Alaska Indian * * * Eskimo, or Aleut blood, or combination thereof."); *id.* § 1604(a) (directing the Secretary of the Interior to prepare a roll of all Alaskan Natives). The Supreme Court has never questioned the authority of Congress to enact such legislation. *See Alaska v. Native Village of Venetie, supra;*
Morton v. Ruiz, 415 U.S. 199, 212 (1974) (quoting passage of Brief for Petitioner the Secretary of the Interior referring to "Indians in Alaska and Oklahoma"); *see also Pence v. Kleppe,* 529 F.2d 135, 138 n.5 (9th Cir. 1976) (when the term "Indians" appears in federal statutes, that word "as applied in Alaska, includes Aleuts and Eskimos"). If Congress has authority to enact special legislation dealing with Native Alaskans, it follows that Congress has the same authority with respect to Native Hawaiians.

Finally, the history of the Hawaiian people confirms that the story of the Hawaiian people, although unique in some respects, is in other ways very similar to the story of all Native Americans. By the time Captain Cook, the first white traveler to Hawaii, "made landfall in Hawaii on his expedition in 1778, the Hawaiian people had developed, over the preceding 1,000 years or so, a cultural and political structure of their own. They had well-established traditions and customs and practiced a polytheistic religion." *Rice,* 528 U.S. at 500. Hawaiian society, the

Court noted, was one "with its own identity, its own cohesive forces, its own history." *Id.* As late as 1810, "the islands were united as one kingdom under the leadership of an admired figure in Hawaiian history, Kamehameha I." *Id.* at 501. King Kamehameha had united the islands and "reasserted suzerainty over all lands." *Id.*

The Nineteenth Century is "a story of increasing involvement of westerners in the economic and political affairs of the Kingdom." *Id.* During this period, the United States established a government-to-government relationship with the Kingdom of Hawaii. Between 1826 and 1887, the two nations executed a number of treaties and conventions. *See id.* at 504.

In 1893, "a group of professionals and businessmen, with the active assistance of John Stevens, the United States Minister to Hawaii, acting with the United States Armed Forces, replaced the monarchy [of Queen Liliuokalani] with a provisional government." *Id.* at 505. In 1894, the U.S.-created provisional government then established the Republic of Hawaii. *See id.* In 1898, President McKinley signed the Newlands Resolution, which annexed Hawaii as a U.S. territory. *See id.*; Territory of Hawaii v. Mankichi, 190 U.S. 197, 209-211 (1903) (discussing the annexation of Hawaii); *Lara*, 541 U.S. at 203-204 (citing the annexation of Hawaii as an example of Congress' adjustment of the autonomous status of a dependent sovereign).

Under the instrument of annexation, the so-called Newlands Resolution, the Republic of Hawaii ceded all public lands to the United States, and the revenue from such lands was to be "used solely for the benefit of the inhabitants of the Hawaiian Islands for educational and other public purposes." *Rice*, 528 U.S. at 505. In 1921, concerned about the deteriorating conditions of the Native Hawaiian people, Congress passed the Hawaiian Homes Commission Act, "which set aside about 200,000 acres of the ceded public lands and created a program of loans and long-term leases for the benefit of native Hawaiians." *Id.* at 507.

In 1959, Hawaii became the 50th State of the United States. *See id.* In connection with its admission to the Union, Hawaii agreed to adopt the Hawaiian Homes Commission Act as part of the Hawaii Constitution, and the United States adopted legislation transferring title to some 1.4 million acres of public lands in Hawaii to the new State, which lands and the revenues they generated were by law to be held "as a public trust" for, among other purposes, "the betterment of the conditions of Native Hawaiians." *Id.* (quoting Admission Act, Pub. L. No. 86-3, § 5(f), 73 Stat. 5, 6).

In short, the story of the Native Hawaiian people is the story of an indigenous people having a distinct culture, religion, and government. Contact with the West brought decimation of the native population through foreign diseases; a period of government-to-government treaty making with the United States; the involvement of the U.S. Government in overthrowing the Native Hawaiian government; the establishment of the public trust relationship between the U.S. Government and Native Hawaiians; and, finally, political union with the United States. Given the parallels between the history of Native Hawaiians and other Native Americans, Congress has ample basis to conclude that it has the coterminous power to deal with the Native Hawaiian community as it has to deal with American Indian tribes. *Cf. Long*, 324 F.3d at 482 ("This case does not involve a people unknown to history before Congress intervened. * * * [W]e have no doubt about congressional power to recognize an ancient group of people for what they are.").[12]

Finally, Congress has found that Native Hawaiians through the present day have maintained a link to the Native Hawaiians who exercised sovereign authority in the past; have never abandoned their claim to be a sovereign people; and have maintained a distinct cultural and social identity. *See* NHGRA § 2(13) ("[T]he Native Hawaiian people never directly relinquished to the United States their claims to their inherent sovereignty as people over their national lands, either through the Kingdom of Hawaii or through a plebiscite or referendum."); *Id.* § 2(15) ("Native Hawaiians have continued to maintain their separate identity as a distinct native community through cultural, social, and political institutions"); *Id.* § 2(22)(A) ("Native Hawaiians have a cultural, historic, and land-based link to the aboriginal, indigenous, native people who exercised sovereignty over the Hawaiian Islands"); *id.* § 2(22)(B); *see also* U.S. Department of Justice & U.S. Department of the Interior, *From Mauka to Makai: The River of Justice Must Flow Freely*, Report on the Reconciliation Process Between the Federal Government and Native Hawaiians at 4 (Oct. 23, 2000) (finding that "the Native Hawaiian people continue to maintain a distinct community and certain governmental structures and they desire to increase their control over their own affairs and institutions").

In 1993, a century after the Kingdom of Hawaii was replaced with the active involvement of the U.S. Minister and the American military, "Congress passed a Joint Resolution recounting the events in some detail and offering an apology to the native Hawaiian people." *Rice*, 528 U.S. at 505. *See* Apology Resolution, Pub. L. No. 103-150, 107 Stat. 1510 (1993). In the Apology Resolution, Congress both "acknowledge[d] the historical significance of this event which resulted in the suppression of the inherent sovereignty of the Native Hawaiian people" and issued a formal apology to Native Hawaiians "for the overthrow of the Kingdom of Hawaii on January 17, 1893 with the participation of agents and citizens of the United States, and the deprivation of the rights of Native Hawaiians to self-determination." *Id.* §§ 1, 3, 107 Stat. 1513.

C. The Responsibility of the U.S. Government for Contributing to the Overthrow of the Hawaiian Kingdom Reinforces Congress' Moral and Legal Authority to Enact the NHGRA

Congress' moral and legal authority to establish a process for the reorganization of the Native Hawaiian governing entity also derives from the role played by the United States -- in particular the U.S. Minister to Hawaii, John Stevens, aided by American military forces -- in bringing a forcible end to the Kingdom of Hawaii in 1893.

---

12 In *Montoya v. United States*, 180 U.S. 261, 266 (1901), the Supreme Court stated that "[b]y a 'tribe' we understand a body of Indians of the same or a similar race, united in a community under one leadership or government, and inhabiting a particular though sometimes ill-defined territory." In so stating, the Court in *Montoya* did not intend to, and did not, circumscribe Congress' authority to recognize Indian tribes. In any event, the community of Native Hawaiian people fit within the *Montoya* definition of a tribe: Native Hawaiians were, and are, of a "same or similar" race, had a unitary governmental system prior to is overthrow, and have inhabited the Hawaiian Islands.

As Congress recounted in the Apology Resolution, the U.S. Minister to the sovereign and independent Kingdom of Hawaii in January 1893 "conspired with a small group of non-Hawaiian residents of the Kingdom of Hawaii, including citizens of the United States, to overthrow the indigenous and lawful Government of Hawaii." 107 Stat. 1510. In pursuit of that objective, U.S. Minister Stevens "and the naval representatives of the United States caused armed naval forces of the United States to invade the sovereign Hawaii nation on January 16, 1893, and to position themselves near the Hawaiian Government buildings and the Iolani Palace to intimidate Queen Liliuokalani and her Government." *Id. See also* S. Rep. No. 108-85, 108th Cong., 2d Sess. 11 (2003) (on the orders of the U.S. Minister, "American soldiers marched through Honolulu, to a building known as Ali'iolani Hale, located near both the government building and the palace"); *Rice*, 528 U.S. at 504-505. The next day, the Queen issued a statement indicating that she would yield her authority "to the superior force of the United States of America whose Minister Plenipotentiary, His Excellency John L. Stevens, has caused United States troops to be landed at Honolulu." 107 Stat. 1511. The United States, quite simply, effected regime change in Hawaii because "without the active support and intervention by the United States diplomatic and military representatives, the insurrection against the Government of Queen Liliuokalani would have failed for lack of popular support and insufficient arms." *Id.* In December 18, 1893, President Cleveland described the Queen's overthrow "as an 'act of war,' committed with the participation of a diplomatic representative of the United States and without the authority of Congress." *Id.*

Given the role of United States agents in the overthrow of the Kingdom of Hawaii, Congress could conclude that its "unique obligation toward the Indians," *Morton v. Mancari*, 417 U.S. at 555, extends to Native Hawaiians. Congress' power to enact special legislation dealing with native people of America is derived from the Constitution, "both explicitly and implicitly." *Id.* at 551 (emphasis added). *See Lara*, 541 U.S. at 201 (to the extent that, through the late 19th Century, Indian affairs were a feature of American military and foreign policy, "Congress' legislative authority would rest in part * * * upon the Constitution's adoption of preconstitutional powers necessarily inherent in any Federal Government"). The Supreme Court has explained that the United States has a special obligation toward the Indians -- a native people who were overcome by force -- and that this obligation carries with it the authority to legislate with the welfare of Indians in mind. As the Court said in *Board of County Commissioners of Creek County v. Seber*, 318 U.S. 705 (1943):

> From almost the beginning the existence of federal power to regulate and protect the Indians and their property against interference even by a state has been recognized. This power is not expressly granted in so many words by the Constitution, except with respect to regulating commerce with the Indian tribes, but its existence cannot be doubted. In the exercise of the war and treaty powers, the United States overcame the Indians and took possession of their lands, sometimes by force, leaving them an uneducated, helpless and dependent people needing protection against the selfishness of others and their own improvidence. Of necessity the United States assumed the duty of furnishing that protection and with it the authority to do all that was required to perform that obligation * * *.

Id. at 715 (citation omitted).

In the case of Native Hawaiians, the maneuverings of the U.S. Minister and the expression of U.S. military force contributed to the overthrow of the Kingdom of Hawaii and the deposition of her Queen. The events of 1893 cannot be undone; but their import extends to this day, imbuing Congress with a special obligation and the inherent authority to restore some semblance of the self-determination then stripped from Native Hawaiians. In the words of Justice Jackson,

> The generation of Indians who suffered the privations, indignities, and brutalities of the westward march of the whites have gone to the Happy Hunting Ground, and nothing that we can do can square the account with them. Whatever survives is a moral obligation resting on the descendants of the whites to do for the descendants of the Indians what in the conditions of this twentieth century is the decent thing.

Northwestern Bands of Shoshone Indians v. United States, 324 U.S. 335, 355 (1945) (concurring opinion).

IV. As an Exercise of Congress' Indian Affairs Powers, the NHGRA Is Not an Impermissible Classification Violative of Equal Protection

The principal objection to the NHGRA -- that it classifies U.S. citizens on the basis of race, in violation of the constitutional guarantee of equal protection, *cf. Rice v. Cayetano*, *supra*,[13] misses the mark. Because the NHGRA is an exercise of Congress' Indian affairs powers, this legislation is "political rather than racial in nature." *Morton v. Mancari*, 417 U.S. at 553 n.24. As the Court explained,

> The decisions of this Court leave no doubt that federal legislation with respect to Indian tribes, although relating to Indians as such, is not based upon impermissible racial classifications. Quite the contrary, classifications expressly singling out Indian tribes as subjects of legislation are expressly provided for in the Constitution and supported by the ensuing history of the Federal Government's relations with Indians. * * * Federal regulation of Indian tribes * * * is governance of once-sovereign political communities; it is not to be viewed as legislation of a " 'racial' group consisting of Indians . . . ." *Morton v. Mancari*, *supra*, at 553 n.24.

United States v. Antelope, 430 U.S. at 645-646 (footnote omitted); *see also Washington v. Confederated Bands & Tribes of the Yakima Indian Nation*, 439 U.S. 463, 500-501 (1979) ("It is settled that 'the unique legal status of Indian tribes under federal law' permits the Federal Government to enact legislation singling out tribal Indians, legislation that might otherwise be constitutionally offensive.") (quoting *Morton v. Mancari*, 417 U.S. at 551-552).

---

13 *Rice* does not support this objection. There, the Court held that the Fifteenth Amendment to the Constitution -- which states that the right of U.S. citizens to vote shall not be denied or abridged by the United States or by any state on account of race or color -- did not allow the State of Hawaii to limit to Native Hawaiians eligibility to vote in elections to elect trustees for the Office of Hawaiian Affairs, a state governmental agency. *See Rice*, 528 U.S. at 523-524. *Rice* is inapposite because the reorganized Native Hawaiian governing entity will be neither a United States nor a Hawaiian governmental entity, but rather the governing entity of a sovereign native people.

In *Morton v. Mancari*, the Supreme Court rejected the claim that an Act of Congress according an employment preference for qualified Indians in the Bureau of Indian Affairs violated the Due Process Clause and federal antidiscrimination provisions. In rejecting that claim, the Court explained that "[o]n numerous occasions this Court specifically has upheld legislation that singles out Indians for particular and special treatment," 417 U.S. at 554 (citing cases involving, *inter alia*, the grant of tax immunity and tribal court jurisdiction), and the Court laid down the following rule with respect to Congress' special treatment of Indians: "As long as the special treatment can be tied rationally to the fulfillment of Congress' unique obligation toward the Indians, such legislative judgments will not be disturbed." *Id.* Clearly, the NHGRA can be "rationally tied" to Congress' discharge of its duty with respect to the native people of Hawaii.

In any event, Native Hawaiians have been denied some of the self-governance authority long established for other indigenous populations in the United States. As Governor Lingle testified to Congress,

> The United States is inhabited by three indigenous peoples -- American Indians, Native Alaskans and Native Hawaiians. * * * Congress has given two of these three populations full self-governance rights. * * * To withhold recognition of the Native Hawaiian people therefore amounts to discrimination since it would continue to treat the nation's three groups of indigenous people differently. * * * [T]oday there is no one governmental entity able to speak for or represent Native Hawaiians. The [NHGRA] would finally allow the process to begin that would bring equal treatment to the Native Hawaiian people.

Testimony of Linda Lingle, Governor of the State of Hawaii, Senate Indian Affairs Committee Hearing on S. 147, at 2 (March 1, 2005) (prepared text). *See also* Statement of Sen. Byron Dorgan, Vice Chairman, Senate Indian Affairs Committee Hearing on S. 147, at 1 (March 1, 2005) ("[T]hrough this bill, the Native Hawaiian people simply seek a status under Federal law that is equal to that of America's other Native peoples -- American Indians and Alaska Natives.") (prepared text); Haunani Apoliona, Chairperson, Board of Trustees, Office of Hawaiian Affairs, Senate Indian Affairs Committee Hearing on S. 147, at 2 (March 1, 2005) ("In this legislation, as Hawaiians, we seek only what long ago was granted this nation's other indigenous peoples.") (prepared text).

* * *

The Supreme Court has confirmed that Congress has broad, plenary constitutional authority to recognize indigenous governments and to help restore and restructure indigenous governments overtly terminated or effectively decimated in earlier eras. See Lara, 541 U.S. at 203 (affirming that the Constitution authorizes Congress "to enact legislation * * * recogniz[ing] * * * the existence of individual tribes" and "restor[ing] previously extinguished tribal status"). That authority extends to the Native Hawaiian people and permits Congress to adopt the NHGRA, which would recognize the Native Hawaiian governing entity and initiate a process for its restoration.

Dissenting Statement of Commissioner Michael J. Yaki
Commissioner Arlan D. Melendez joins in this dissent.

Preface

As a person quite possibly with native Hawaiian blood running through his veins,[14] it is quite possible to say that I cannot possibly be impartial when it comes to this issue. And, in truth, that may indeed be the fact. Nevertheless, even before my substantive objections are made known, from a process angle there were serious and substantial flaws in the methodology underlying the report.

First, the report relies upon a briefing from a grand total of four individuals, on an issue that has previously relied upon months of research and fact gathering that has led to two State Advisory Commission reports, one Department of Justice Report, and Congressional action (the "Apology Resolution"), not to mention testimony before the Congress on the NHGRA bill itself that was never incorporated into the record.

The paucity of evidence adduced is hardly the stuff upon which to make recommendations or findings. Even though the Commission, to its credit, stripped the report of all its findings for its final version, does that not itself lend strength and credence to the suggestion that the briefing was flawed from the inception? And if so flawed, how can the Commission opine so strongly upon a record that it could not even find supported now non-existent findings?

Second, aside from ignoring the volumes of research and testimony that lie elsewhere and easily available to the Commission, we ignored soliciting advice and comment from our own State Advisory Commission of Hawai'i. Over the past two decades, the Hawai'i Advisory Committee to the United States Commission on Civil Rights ("HISAC") has examined issues relating to federal and state relations with Native Hawaiians. As early as 1991, HISAC recommended legislation confirming federal recognition of Native Hawaiians. A mere five years ago, the HISAC found that "the lack of federal recognition for native Hawaiians appears to constitute a clear case of discrimination among the native peoples found within the borders of this nation."[15] The HISAC concluded "[a]bsent explicit recognition of a Native Hawaiian governing entity, or at least a process for ultimate recognition thereof, it is clear that the civil and political rights of Native Hawaiians will continue to erode."[16] The HISAC found that "the denial of Native Hawaiian self-determination and self-governance to be a serious erosion of this group's equal protection and human rights."[17] Echoing recommendations by the United States

---

14 My grandfather was born in Hana, Maui, and placed in an orphanage. The story passed down was that he was the product of a Japanese laborer on the islands and a Native Hawaiian. The orphanage records burned down some time ago, so we are unable to verify for sure whether he was half-native Hawaiian or not, but for anyone who knew or saw my grandfather, he had many Polynesian physical characteristics.
15 Hawaii Advisory Committee to the U.S. Commission on Civil Rights, *Reconciliation at a Crossroads: The Implications of the Apology Resolution and Rice v. Cayetano for Federal and State Programs Benefiting Native Hawaiians*, at ix (June 2001).
16 *Id.* at 49.
17 *Id.*

Departments of Justice and Interior, the HISAC "strongly recommend[ed]" that the federal government "accelerate efforts to formalize the political relationship between Native Hawaiians and the United States."[18] The HISAC's long-standing position of support for legislation like S. 147 to protect the civil rights of native Hawaiians belies recent assertions that such legislation discriminates on the basis of race and causes further racial divide.

The HISAC could and would have been a key source of information, especially updated information, on the state of the record. To exclude them from the dialogue I believe was indefensible and a deliberate attempt to ensure that contrary views were not introduced into the record.

Third, the report as it stands now makes no sense. The lack of findings, the lack of any factual analysis, now makes the report the proverbial Emperor without clothes. The conclusion of the Commission stands without support, without backing, and will be looked upon, I believe, as irrelevant to the debate. Such is the risk one runs when scholarship and balance are lacking.

Substantively, the recommendation of the Commission cannot stand either. It is not based on facts about the political status of indigenous, Native Hawaiians; nor Native Hawaiian history and governance; or facts about existing U.S. policy and law concerning Native Hawaiians. It is a misguided attempt to start a new and destructive precedent in U.S. policy toward Native Americans. The USCCR recommendation disregards the U.S. Constitution that specifically addresses the political relationship between the U.S. and the nations of Native Americans. The USCCR disregarded facts when the choice was made not to include HISAC in the January 2006 briefing on NHGRA and not utilizing the past relevant HISAC reports concerning Native Hawaiians based on significant public hearing and facts. Spring-boarding from trick phrasing and spins offered by ill informed experts, at least one of whom has filed suit to end Native Hawaiian programs established through Congress and the state constitution, the USCCR majority recommendation is an obvious attempt to treat Native Hawaiians unfairly in order to begin the process of destroying existing U.S. policy towards Native Americans.

Facts About Indigenous Native Hawaiians, Native Hawaiian and U.S. History, and the Distinct Native Hawaiian Indigenous Political Community Today

Native Hawaiians are the indigenous people of Hawai'i, just as American Indians and Alaska Natives are the indigenous peoples of the remaining 49 states. Hawai'i is the homeland of Native Hawaiians. Over 1,200 years prior to the arrival of European explorer James Cook on the Hawaiian islands, Native Hawaiians determined their own form of governance, culture, way of life, priorities and economic system in order to cherish and protect their homelands, of which they are physically and spiritually a part. They did so continuously until the illegal overthrow of their government by agents and citizens of the U.S. government in 1893. In fact the U.S. engaged in several treaties and conventions with the Native Hawaiian government, including 1826, 1842, 1849, 1875 and 1887. Though deprived of their inherent rights to self-determination as a direct result of the illegal overthrow, coupled with subsequent efforts to terminate Native Hawaiian language, leaders, institutions and government functions, Native Hawaiians persevered

---

18 *Id.*

as best they could to perpetuate the distinct vestiges of their culture, institutions, homelands and government functions in order to maintain a distinct community, recognizable to each other.

Today, those living in Hawai'i recognize these aspects of the distinct, functioning Native Hawaiian political community easily. For example: the Royal Benevolent Societies established by Ali'i (Native Hawaiian chiefs and monarchs) continue to maintain certain Native Hawaiian government assigned and cultural functions; the private Ali'i Trusts, such as Kamehameha Schools, Queen Lili'uokalani Trust, Queen Emma Foundation and Lunalilo Home, joined by state government entities established for indigenous Hawaiians, including the Office of Hawaiian Affairs and the Department of Hawaiian Homelands, and Native Hawaiian Serving institutions such as Alu Like, Inc. and Queen Lili'uokalani Children's Center continue the Native Hawaiian government functions of caring for Native Hawaiian health, orphans and families, education, elders, housing economic development, governance, community wide communication and culture and arts; the resurgence of teaching and perpetuation of Native Hawaiian language and other cultural traditions; Native Hawaiian civic participation in matters important to the Native Hawaiian community are conducted extensively through Native Hawaiian organizations including the Association of Hawaiian Civic Clubs, the State Council of Hawaiian Homestead Associations, the Council for Native Hawaiian Advancement, Ka Lahui and various small groups pursuing independence; and Native Hawaiian family reunions where extended family members, young and old, gather to talk, eat, pass on family stories and history, sometimes sing and play Hawaiian music and dance hula and pass on genealogy.

Indeed, if the briefing had been as consultative with the HISAC as it could have been, there would have been testimony that, for example, the Royal Order of Kamehameha, the Hale O Na Ali'I o Hawai'I, and the Daughters of Ka'ahumanu continue to operate under principles consistent with the law of the former Kingdom of Hawai'i. There would have been testimony that these groups went "underground" due to persecution but remained very much alive during that time.[19]

The distinct indigenous, political community of Native Hawaiians is recognized by Congress in over 150 pieces of legislation, including the Hawaiian Homes Commission Act and the conditions of statehood. Native Hawaiians are recognized as a distinct indigenous, political community by voters of Hawai'i, as expressed in the Hawai'i state constitution.

The notion introduced by opponents to the NHGRA that the Native Hawaiians don't "fit" federal regulations governing recognition of Native American tribes because they lacked a distinct political identity or continuous functional and separate government[20] would ignore all the manifestations of such identity, existence, and recognition noted above.

---

19 Communication from Quentin Kawananakoa, former member of the Hawai'i State Advisory Committee, May 12, 2006.
20 See 25 C.F.R. §83.

The NHGRA Does Not Set New Precedent in U.S.

The NHGRA is in fact a measure to establish fairness in U.S. policy towards the three groups of Native Americans of the 50 united states—American Indians, Alaska Natives and Native Hawaiians. The U.S. already provides American Indians and Alaska Natives access to a process of federal recognition, and the NHGRA does the same for Native Hawaiians based on the same constitutional and statutory standing.

I. Legal Authorities Establishing OHA/ Purpose of OHA

Hawai'i became the fiftieth state in the union in 1959 pursuant to Pub. L. No. 86-3, 73 Stat. 5 ("Admission Act"). Under this federal law, the United States granted the nascent state title to all public lands within the state, except for some lands reserved for use by the federal Government ("public lands trust"). These lands "together with the proceeds from the sale or other disposition of any such lands and the income therefrom, shall be held by [the State] as a public trust for the support of the public schools, . . . the conditions of native Hawaiians" and other purposes.[21]

In 1978, the multicultural residents of Hawai'i voted to amend its state Constitution to 1) establish the Office of Hawaiian Affairs ("OHA") to "provide Hawaiians the right to determine the priorities which will effectuate the betterment of their condition and welfare and promote the protection and preservation of the Hawaiian race, and . . . [to] unite Hawaiians as a people;"[22] and 2) to establish the public lands trust created by the Admission Act as a constitutional obligation of the State of Hawaii to the native people.[23]

The constitutional mandate for OHA was implemented in 1979 via the enactment of Chapter 10, Hawaii Revised Statutes. OHA's statutory purposes include "[a]ssessing the policies and practices of other agencies impacting on native Hawaiians and Hawaiians," conducting advocacy efforts for native Hawaiians and Hawaiians," "[a]pplying for, receiving, and disbursing, grants and donations from all sources for native Hawaiian and Hawaiian programs and services," and "[s]erving as a vehicle for reparations."[24] OHA administers funds derived for the most part from its statutory 20-percent share of revenues generated by the use of the public lands trust.[25]

Several legal challenges to the existence of OHA based upon the Fourteenth Amendment to the United States Constitution have been filed by various plaintiffs, some of who are represented by Mr. Burgess. Mr. Burgess has thus far failed to win the relief he has sought, including injunctive relief, either in the United States District Court for the District of Hawaii or the United States Court of Appeals for the Ninth Circuit. The denial of injunctive relief to Mr.

---

21 § 5 (f), 73 Stat. 6.

22 1 Proceedings of the Constitutional Convention of Hawai'i 1978, Committee of the Whole Rep. 13, p. 1018 (1980)

23 William Burgess, who testified at the briefing, was a delegate to the 1978 Constitutional Convention, yet Mr. Burgess then voiced no opposition to the establishment of OHA. Communication of Martha Ross, Office of Hawaiian Affairs, May 2006.

24 HRS § 10-3 (4)-(6).

25 HRS § 10-13.5.

Burgess's clients presents a powerful rebuttal to their claims that OHA's administration of its constitutional and statutory obligations to native Hawaiians and Hawaiians deprives all Hawaii's citizens of equal protection of law.

Mr. Burgess describes the "driving force" behind the NHGRA as "discrimination based upon ancestry." Nothing could be further from the truth or more illogical. The "driving force" behind the creation and passage of NHGRA is the desire of the Hawaiian people, and virtually every political representative in the State of Hawaii to achieve federal recognition and legal parity with federal recognition as with the other two native indigenous peoples of America, namely American Indian Nations and Native Alaskans. There is no constitutional impediment to congressional federal recognition of the Hawaiian people.[26]

Then-United States Solicitor John Roberts (now Chief Justice Roberts) argued in his prior legal briefs to the United States Supreme Court in *Rice v. Cayetano*: "[T]he Constitution, in short, gives Congress room to deal with the particular problems posed by the indigenous people of Hawaii and, at least when legislation is in furtherance of the obligation Congress has assumed to those people, that legislation is no more racial in nature than legislation attempting to honor the federal trust responsibility to any other indigenous people." It is, in sum, "not racial at all."

Roberts went on to say:

Congress is constitutionally empowered to deal with Hawaiians, has recognized such a "special relationship," and—"[i]n recognition of th[at] special relationship"--has extended to Native Hawaiians the same rights and privileges accorded to American Indian, Alaska Native, Eskimo, and Aleut communities." 20 U.S.C. § 7902(13) (emphasis added). As such, Congress has established with Hawaiians the same type of "unique legal relationship" that exists with respect to the Indian tribes who enjoy the "same rights and privileges" accorded Hawaiians under these laws. 42 U.S.C. § 11701(19). That unique legal or political status--not recognition of "tribal" status, under the latest executive transmutation of what that means--is the touchstone for application of Mancari when, as here, Congress is constitutionally empowered to treat an indigenous group as such.

NHGRA Is a Matter of Indigenous Political Status and Relationship Between the U.S. and the Native Hawaiian Government, and Not a Racial Matter.

Under the U.S. Constitution and federal law, America's indigenous, native people are recognized as groups that are not defined by race or ethnicity, but by the fact that their indigenous, native ancestors exercised sovereignty over the lands and areas that subsequently became part of the United States. It is the pre-existing sovereignty—sovereignty that pre-existed the formation of the United States—which the U.S. Constitution recognizes and, on that basis, accords a special status to America's indigenous, native people.

The tortured attempts by persons such as Mr. Burgess to distinguish Native Hawaiians from Native Americans ultimately fail by simple historical comparison. Like the Native

---

26 *See U.S. v. Lara.* 541 U.S. 193 (2004).

Americans, the Native Hawaiians pre-dated the establishment of the United States. Like the Native Americans, the Native Hawaiians had their own culture, form of government, and distinct sense of identity. Like Native Americans, the United States stripped them of the ownership of their land and trampled over their sovereignty. The only distinction – one without a difference –- is that unlike the vast majority of Native American tribes, the Native Hawaiians were not shipped off, force-marched, and relocated to another area far from their original homelands.[27]

It is somewhat disingenuous that the opponents of NHGRA are suggesting that extending this same U.S. policy to Native Hawaiians, the indigenous, native people of the fiftieth state would lead to racial balkanization. There are over 560 federally recognized American Indian and Alaska Native governing entities in 49 of 50 states, coexisting with all peoples and federal, state and local governments. There is absolutely NO evidence to support this notion, and seems to be spread simply to instill unwarranted fear and opposition to the NHGRA.

NHGRA is Constitutional

In *United States v. Lara*, the Supreme Court held that "[t]he Constitution grants Congress broad general powers to legislate in respect to Indian tribes powers that we have consistently described as plenary and exclusive." In 1954, Congress terminated the sovereignty of the Menominee Indian Tribe in Wisconsin. In 1973, Congress exercised its discretion, changed its mind, and enacted the Menominee Restoration Act, which restored sovereignty to the Menominee Tribe.

NHGRA does little more than follow the precedent allowed by *Lara* and exercised in the Menominee case. Reliance on federal regulations as gospel ignores the fact that the plenary authority of Congress has resulted in restoration of tribal status, in the case of the Menominee, and the retroactive restoration of tribal lands, as in the case of the Lytton Band in California. The Attorney General of Hawaii, many distinguished professors, and the American Bar Association all firmly believe that Congress has the authority to recognize Native Hawaiians.[28]

All that NHGRA seeks is parity in U.S. policies towards the three indigenous, native people in the 50 states, American Indians, Alaska Natives and Native Hawaiians. Under the U.S. Constitution and Federal law, America's indigenous, native people are recognized as groups that

---

27 Although, like Native Americans, the land ceded to them under the Hawaiian Homes Act is, for the most part, largely uninhabitable or not readily susceptible to development.

28 On February 13, 2006, the policy-making body of the 400,000 members American Bar Association (ABA) "… voted overwhelmingly in favor of a resolution to urge Congress to pass legislation to establish a process to provide federal recognition for a Native Hawaiian governing entity. Such legislation, S. 147, proposed by Sen. Daniel Akaka, is currently pending in Congress." As further explained by Alan Van Etten, Hawai'i state delegate, ABA, in a Letter to the Editor published on February 21, 2006 in the Honolulu Advertiser, " …The ABA's mission is to be the national representative of the legal profession, serving the public and the profession by promoting justice, professional excellence and respect for the law. By passing the resolution, the delegates said yes to the establishment by Congress of a process that would provide Native Hawaiians the same status afforded to America's other indigenous groups, American Indians and Native Alaskans. The blessing by this country's largest and most prestigious legal organization would appear to put to rest the primary legal arguments advanced by this bill's opponents. … The American Bar Association's support for Hawai'i's indigenous people sends a strong message that a process for Native Hawaiian recognition follows the rule of law and provides great impetus for Congress to take immediate action to pass the Akaka bill."

are not defined by race or ethnicity, but by the fact that their indigenous, native ancestors, exercised sovereignty over the lands and areas that subsequently became part of the United States. It is the pre-existing sovereignty, sovereignty that pre-existed the formation of the United States which the U.S. Constitution recognizes and on that basis, accords a special status to America's indigenous, native people.

If one accepts the Commission's pronouncement against subdividing the country into "discrete subgroups accorded varying degrees of privilege," then the Commission should immediately call for an end to any recognition of additional Indian tribes. Since that would clearly contravene the Constitutional authority of Congress, that would seem to be an unlikely— and illegal—outcome. Given that the authority for NHGRA stems from the same constitutional source as that for Native Americans, then the Commission majority has chosen to ignore the constitutionality of the proposed law.

NHGRA Has the Support of the Residents of Hawai'i as Reflected in Two Scientific Polls, the Fact that the Majority of Officials Elected by the Voters of Hawai'i Support NHGRA.

The results of a scientific poll in Hawai'i showed 68 percent of those surveyed support the bill.[29] The statewide poll was taken Aug. 15-18 by Ward Research, a local public opinion firm. [30] The results are consistent with a 2003 poll.[31] While polls alone do not a mandate make, the consistency between the two polls shows that despite the best efforts of opponents such as Mr. Burgess, the multicultural, multiethnic residents of Hawaii support the recognition of Native Hawaiians and would allow them to take the first, tentative, steps toward recognition and sovereignty.

More importantly, the elected officials of Hawaii have almost unanimously thrown their support to the NHGRA. The NHGRA is supported by most of the elected officials of Hawai'i, including the entire Hawai'i Congressional Delegation, Governor Linda Lingle, the Senate and House of the State Legislature (except two members), all nine Trustees of the Office of Hawaiian Affairs and the mayors of all four counties of Hawai'i.

Conclusion

The NHGRA is about justice. It is about righting a wrong. It is about recognition of the identity and sovereignty of a people who survived attempts by our government to strip them of these precious rights over a hundred years ago. Far from the racial balkanization spread by its

---

29 *OHA Poll Shows Strong Community Support for Akaka Bill*, HONOLULU STAR BULLETIN, August 23, 2005.
30 OHA paid for the poll of 401 randomly selected Hawai'i residents, which had a margin of error of plus or minus 4.9 percentage points.
31 *OHA Poll Finds Public Favors Federal Recognition*, HONOLULU ADVERTISER, October 24, 2003. Ward Research was hired in July of 2003 to conduct the telephone survey, in which 600 residents were contacted, about half of them Native Hawaiians. Federal recognition won support from 86 percent of the Hawaiian survey bloc, and 78 percent of the non-Hawaiian participants. However, the idea of creating a Hawaiian government drew 72 percent support from Hawaiian participants and 53 percent from non-Hawaiians.

opponents, NHGRA is simply a step – a baby step at that – towards potential limited sovereignty and self-governance.

Most who live in Hawai'i know the distinct Native Hawaiian community, with its own language and culture, is the heart and breath of Hawai'i. Hawai'i, and no other place on earth, is the homeland of Native Hawaiians.

On one thing the proponents and opponents of NHGRA seem to agree: Hawai'i is a special place in these United States, a multicultural society and model for racial and ethnic harmony that is unlike anywhere else in our country and, increasingly, the world. It is also a place where its multicultural residents recognize the indigenous Native Hawaiian culture as the host culture with a special indigenous political status where there are state holidays acknowledging Native Hawaiian monarchs, and the Hawaiian language is officially recognized.

Perhaps it is the "mainlanders" lack of context and experience that creates a debate where, in Hawai'i, there is practically none. In the mainland, we think of "Aloha" as Hawaii Five-O, surfing, and brightly colored shirts that remain tucked away in the back of our closets. In Hawai'i, however, *Aloha* and the *Aloha* spirit is more than just a slogan. It is proof positive of the influence and power of the Native Hawaiian people and culture that exists and thrives today. In my lifetime, I have seen growing awareness, acceptance and usage of Hawaiian culture, symbols, and language. It is now almost mandatory to use pronunciation symbols whenever Hawaiian words are printed, whereas twenty years ago it was ignored. Multiculturalism in modern Hawai'i means that non-Native Hawaiians respect and honor the traditions of a people who settle on these volcanic paradises after braving thousands of miles of open ocean. The least we can do, the "we" being the American government which took away their islands, is to accord them the basic respect, recognition, and privileges we do all indigenous peoples of our nation. NHGRA will give meaning to the Apology Resolution; it will begin the healing of wounds.

That same *aloha* spirit that imbues the multicultural islands of Hawai'i will, in my opinion, ensure that the processes contained in NHGRA will inure to the benefit of all the people of Hawaii. Perhaps more than any other place in our Union, fears of racial polarization, discrimination, or unequal treatment resulting from the passage of NHGRA should be seen as distant as the stars which the Hawaiians used to navigate their *wa'a*, their canoes, across the vastness of the seas.

Dissenting Statement of Commissioner Arlan D. Melendez
Commissioner Michael J. Yaki joins in this dissent.

In 1893, shortly after becoming President, Grover Cleveland appointed a special envoy to Hawai'i, James Blount, to investigate the circumstances of the overthrow of the indigenous Hawaiian government and the standing of the Provisional Government. Blount delivered a report to President Cleveland later that year finding that representatives of the United States had abused their authority and their participation in the overthrow was responsible for its success.

On the basis of this report, President Cleveland declared that a "substantial wrong has thus been done which a due regard for our national character as well as the rights of the injured people requires we should endeavor to repair," and called for the restoration of the Hawaiian monarchy. The Senate Foreign Relations Committee, at the behest of the Provisional Government, also investigated the role of the U.S. in the overthrow. The Committee held a series of hearings in which representatives of the Provisional Government were given unfettered access to the process in order to justify and obscure their role and that of the U.S., in what President Cleveland referred to as "an act of war…" against the sovereign Hawaiian nation. The Committee Chair issued his opinion exonerating the U.S. of wrongdoing (now known as the Morgan report), blaming the overthrow on the Native Hawaiian monarch. No other committee members signed the Chair's opinion and four members of the committee vigorously dissented, finding that the diplomatic and military might of the U.S. was misused to overthrow the government of the Hawaiian people.

The Apology Resolution approved by Congress in 1993 (attached) officially adopts the accurate account of the overthrow of Hawaii presented in the Blount report and repudiates the Morgan Report. Once again the United States government has acknowledged that an injustice has been committed that "our national character… requires we should endeavor to repair" and is considering legislation that would set in motion the process of repairing the illegal actions committed by the United States over 100 years ago. Yet, the Commission recommends that Congress should not pass this legislation. Because I believe that with today's action the Commission has become a 21st century Morgan Report, I respectfully dissent.

Discussion

I fear that the Commission has lost sight of the bigger picture in making its recommendation. There is much more at stake in this debate than the passage of a particular bill or how Congress remedies the injustice perpetrated against the Native Hawaiian government. The crux of the issue before us, as I see it, is whether the United States government has a moral obligation and the requisite legal authority, to rectify a wrong it has committed. It is inconceivable to me to suggest that the United States government lacks the legal authority to choose to right a wrong that it admits responsibility for, but this seems to be what some of the opponents of this legislation suggest. Justice and fundamental fairness dictate that the federal government must have this power. To argue otherwise is a perversion of the principles and values that underpin our democracy that I simply cannot abide.

Moreover, I believe there is a moral imperative for the federal government to attempt to make amends for the injustices it has committed. I disagree with the sentiment suggested by several of my colleagues that even if Congress has the power to re-recognize the Native Hawaiian government, to do so would be ill-advised. To echo President Cleveland, I believe our national character requires that we endeavor to repair the wrong we have committed.

The Apology Resolution passed by Congress in 1993 acknowledges that an injustice was perpetrated against the Native Hawaiian government by the United States, and there is real value in the fact of this acknowledgement. An apology implies, however, that there is also a concomitant will to address the ramifications of that injustice. There is a lot of unfinished business that must be attended to before true reconciliation between the United States and the Native Hawaiians can be achieved. For the Apology Resolution to be more than hollow words on paper, Congress must take the next step forward in this reconciliation process. I commend the sponsors and supporters of S. 147 for their efforts to do the right thing.

Turning to the specific remedy Congress has chosen—establishing a process for the reorganization of the indigenous Hawaiian government—I believe that the integrity of the Commission's recommendation would be better served by a rigorous analysis of the principles of federal law that inform the various legislative enactments of the Congress extending federal recognition to certain other groups of indigenous peoples within the United States. In the more than 200 years that the federal government has been dealing with the indigenous peoples of this land, a robust and complex body of law has developed that should inform the Commission's consideration of S. 147. To suggest that Native Hawaiians are situated in some way that is fundamentally different than American Indians and Alaska Natives, and that therefore these principles do not apply, flies in the face of reason and common sense.

Like the other indigenous peoples of the United States, the Native Hawaiians have a history that long pre-dates discovery of their lands by Westerners. Like American Indians and Alaska Natives, Native Hawaiians have experienced a long history of destructive federal policies aimed at eroding their land base, culture, governmental authority, and economies. But, like American Indians and Alaska Natives, the Native Hawaiian culture and community has survived this terrible history, and it is long past time that their right to self-determination be given full effect.

The unique legal and political relationship that indigenous peoples have with the United States is based on our status as aboriginal people with pre-existing governments with whom the U.S. entered treaties and other agreements. It is this historical, political reality that provides the foundation for the unique relationship that has always existed—and continues to exist today—between the United States and the indigenous people whose homelands fall within the borders of the United States.

The principles of federal law that apply to Congressional efforts to address the conditions of the indigenous peoples of the United States have their origin in the U.S. Constitution. One source of such constitutional authority is found in Article I, section 8, clause 3 of the Constitution which provides that, "the Congress shall have the authority to regulate commerce with the several States, foreign nations, and the Indian tribes."

The courts have described Congress's power over Indian affairs as "plenary and exclusive."[32] In one of its most recent rulings, the U.S. Supreme Court has described the dynamic nature of Congress' constitutional authority in the field of Native affairs in this manner, "the Government's Indian policies, applicable to numerous tribes with diverse cultures, affecting billions of acres of land, of necessity would fluctuate dramatically as the needs of the Nation and those of the tribes changed over time," and "such major policy changes inevitably involve major changes in the metes and bounds of tribal sovereignty."[33]

As, over the course of our history, the term "Indians" has been used to describe the indigenous people encountered in geographic areas of the continental United States beyond the original thirteen states that were parties to the first Constitution, including the indigenous native people of Alaska and Hawaii, it is both important and relevant to revisit the origins of this term.

Historical documents and dictionaries make clear that the terms "Indians" and "Indian tribe" were terms derived from commonly-used European parlance which sought to describe the aboriginal, indigenous native people of the various nation states around the world as early as the 1500s. These were never words that the indigenous peoples applied to themselves. The debates of the Continental Congress and the written discourse amongst the Framers of the Constitution as it relates to this provision of the Constitution use the terms "Indians" and "Indian tribes" interchangeably, and it was only in the last draft of the Constitution that emerged from the conference that the term "Indian tribes" was ultimately adopted.

Understanding what is encompassed in these terms is significant for constitutional purposes, because they describe the scope of Congress' authority to enact legislation affecting America's indigenous peoples, notwithstanding the fact that the Congress has from time to time chosen to define the indigenous, native people of the United States by reference to blood quantum or race.[34] And with reference to the issue of the use of blood quantum or race, it is Congress' constitutional authority under the Indian Commerce Clause that has led the Supreme Court to draw a legal distinction between laws enacted for the benefit of America's indigenous, native people and assertions that such laws, such as an Indian employment preference law, constitute racial discrimination. In the landmark case, *Morton v. Mancari*,[35] the U.S. Supreme Court observed:

> Literally every piece of legislation dealing with Indian tribes and reservations, and certainly all legislation dealing with the BIA, single out for special treatment a constituency of tribal Indians living on or near reservations. If these laws, derived from historical relationships and explicitly designed to help only Indians, were deemed invidious racial discrimination, an entire Title of the United States Code (25 U.S.C.) would be effectively erased and the solemn commitment of the Government towards the Indians would be jeopardized.

---

32 *United States v. Lara*, 541 U.S. 193, 200 (2004).
33 *United States v. Lara*, 541 U.S. 193, 200 (2004).
34 Indian Reorganization Act of 1934, 25 U.S.C. § 461, *et seq.*
35 417 U.S. 535, 94 S. Ct. 2474, 41 L.Ed.2d 290 (1974).

On numerous occasions this Court specifically has upheld legislation that singles out Indians for particular and special treatment. This unique status is of long standing....and its sources are diverse. As long as the special treatment can be tied rationally to the fulfillment of Congress' unique obligation toward the Indians, such legislative judgments will not be disturbed. Here, where the preference is reasonable and rationally designed to further Indian self-government, we cannot say that Congress' classification violates due process.

It is within this legal framework that the Congress has enacted legislation to extend federal recognition to various groups of America's indigenous peoples. As Professors Viet Dinh and Christopher Bartolomucci observed in their testimony submitted to the Commission for its January 20, 2006, briefing on S. 147, the U.S. Supreme Court has sustained this exercise of Congress's constitutional authority most recently in 2004 when it –

recognized Congress' power to restore previously extinguished sovereign relations with Indian tribes. The Court observed that 'Congress has restored previously extinguished tribal status – by re-recognizing a Tribe whose tribal existence it previously had terminated.' *Id.* (citing Congress' restoration of the Menominee Tribe in 25 U.S.C. §§ 903-903f). And the Court cited the 1898 annexation of Hawaii as an example of Congress' power "to modify the degree of autonomy enjoyed by a dependent sovereign that is not a State."[36]

The argument that recognition of a Native Hawaiian governing entity would discriminate on the basis of race conflicts with the long-standing principles of federal law concerning the relationship between the United States government's and the indigenous peoples who have inhabited this land from time immemorial—a relationship that has long been recognized by Congress, the federal courts, and the Executive branch. Those making this argument are suggesting that Native Hawaiians should, and indeed must, be treated differently from the other indigenous peoples residing in what is now the United States. S. 147 is intended to establish parity for Native Hawaiians with the other indigenous peoples of America. Those who invoke the equal protection or due process clauses of the Constitution to oppose this legislation are using the very cornerstones of justice and fairness in our democracy to deny equal treatment to one group of indigenous people.

Specific Concerns

I would also like to address some of the specific concerns that were raised by Commissioners at the briefing and during our subsequent discussions.

Constitutional Protections

In the dialogue that took place between Commissioners and those presenting testimony on S. 147 in the January 20, 2006 briefing, there were questions posed with regard to the civil

---

36 *Lara,* 124 S. Ct. at 205.

rights protections that would be afforded by a Native Hawaiian government to its citizens and to others, be they Native Hawaiian or non-Hawaiian, who voluntarily consent to the jurisdiction of the Native Hawaiian government. In this regard, I believe that it is important to understand, as several of the witnesses testified, that the provisions of the U.S. Constitution, including those protections of the amendments to the U.S. Constitution, apply to all acts of the Congress.

Because federal law recognizes Indian tribes as sovereigns that pre-existed the formation of the United States and the U.S. Supreme Court has affirmed that the Indian tribes as sovereigns were not parties to the U.S. Constitution, Congress has enacted laws to extend the protections of many of the Constitution's guarantees to Indian tribes.

In contrast, there is no provision of S. 147 that exempts the Native Hawaiian government from the U.S. Constitution, and thus, the Native Hawaiian government must accord to all who come under the jurisdiction of the Native Hawaiian government all the protections and guarantees of the U.S. Constitution. In certifying that the organic governing documents of the Native Hawaiian government are consistent with applicable federal law, the Secretary of the Interior is required to assure that the organic governing documents are consistent with not only federal statutes but the protections and guarantees of the U.S. Constitution.

Federal Regulations

Over the course of the Commission's deliberations, the suggestion was raised that Native Hawaiians should be required to use the Bureau of Indian Affairs regulatory process for seeking recognition. I would like to clarify that the recognition criteria established by regulation, however, represent only one way that a tribe can seek federal recognition. Tribes have also been recognized by legislation, executive order, and by court decisions. The Indian Commerce Clause gives Congress the authority to recognize groups of Indians as tribes. This Congressional power has been delegated to the Executive branch to take actions consistent with this recognition and it is pursuant to this authority that the recognition criteria mentioned were developed.[37] Clearly, since delegated congressional power provides the basis for the regulatory recognition criteria, Congress retains the power to recognize tribes outside of these criteria as well.

Congress has done just that with regard to certain groups of indigenous, native people of the United States who are not eligible to participate in the federal agency regulatory process– in some instances because the federal recognition of the native group was terminated by action of the Congress, or in other instances, because the native group does not reside within the continental United States. The Native Hawaiian people are a group who come within this latter category. They must pursue the federal recognition of their sovereignty, as given expression through the reorganization of a Native government, through Congressional action, because they are not eligible to participate in the federal regulatory process, by the express terms of the regulations.

---

37 Felix Cohen's Handbook of Federal Indian Law, Sec. 3.02[4] (2005 ed.).

Substitute Amendment

Because the Commission's recommendation is tied to the amendment in the nature of a substitute to S. 147 that was reported by the Senate Indian Affairs Committee on March 9, 2006, it fails to take into consideration the outcome of negotiations that were conducted with representatives of the White House Office of Management and Budget, the Department of Justice and the State of Hawaii and which resulted in further amendments to S. 147.

At its January 20, 2006 briefing, a copy of the substitute amendment to S. 147 containing the negotiated amendments to the bill was provided to the Commissioners by Noe Kalipi, who serves as the Minority Staff Director of the Senate Committee on Veterans Affairs for Senator Akaka and who provided testimony to the Commission at the January 20, 2006 briefing.

Despite the fact that Ms. Kalipi explained that it would be this substitute amendment that would be the subject of the Senate's consideration when S. 147 is taken up in the Senate, the Commissioners voted to base the Commission's recommendation on an earlier, and now superseded version of the bill. Given the participation of representatives of the White House, the Justice Department, and the State of Hawaii in developing the provisions of the substitute amendment, it is my view that the integrity of the Commission's report would have been better served by basing the Commission's finding on the substitute amendment to S. 147.

Other Groups

During the Commission briefing, the question was raised whether groups of illegal or legal immigrants or their descendants with a shared ethnicity, or even a religious group, would be able to claim to be indigenous people and seek special rights. This slippery slope argument is unfounded. Any of these unnamed groups could attempt to seek self-governance rights at any time, regardless of passage of this bill. However, there are a finite number of indigenous groups whose homelands are now within the boundaries of the United States, and it would be impossible for any other racial or ethnic group to fit within the authority given to Congress in the Indian Commerce Clause.

Existence of Native Governments

While the Commission's recommendation against passage of S. 147 suggests that the Native Hawaiian Government Reorganization Act falls within the category of legislation that "would discriminate on the basis of race or national origin and further subdivide the American people into discrete subgroups accorded varying degrees of privilege," I find no evidence in any of the provisions of S. 147 that would support such a conclusion. Nor am I aware of any research into or documentation of Congressional intent that has been undertaken by the Commission that would lend support to the notion that the bill is intended to subdivide discrete subgroups accorded varying degrees of privilege. In fact, I can find no basis for that conclusion in the record of our briefing or subsequent submissions other than assertions of personal opinion.

I respectfully remind my colleagues that in 49 other states indigenous nations have peacefully coexisted with our neighbors for many years. I can think of no reason, nor did we hear any testimony to suggest one, why this would not also be the case in Hawaii. As a tribal leader, I am deeply troubled that the Commission recommendation could be read to suggest that the existence of Indian tribes within the federal system is somehow undesirable and should not be extended to Native Hawaiians.

Conclusion

Native Hawaiians have now suffered more than a century of injustice, and reaffirmation of the inherent Native Hawaiian right to self-governance by the federal government is long overdue. S. 147 will begin the process of righting the wrong committed by the United States against the indigenous Hawaiian government and will help to ensure the preservation of the Hawaiian culture. As President Cleveland said so long ago, I believe that once Congress acknowledged the wrong that had been committed against the Native Hawaiians, our national character compels that we attempt to right that wrong.

It is long past time for the United States to stop ignoring the historic injustices our nation has perpetrated against the indigenous peoples of the United States. If we continue down this path, our standing as a model of justice and equality for the rest of the world will be jeopardized.

For all of the above reasons, I dissent from the Commission's recommendation.

Appendix A

The substitute amendment to S. 147 which was presented to the Commissioners on January 20, 2006 by Ms. Kalipi contains the following provisions –

- clarification that the United States has a special political and legal relationship for the welfare of the native peoples of the United States, including Native Hawaiians;

- clarification that when transferring the federal government's responsibility for the administration of the Hawaiian Home Lands to the State of Hawaii, the United States retained the exclusive right to consent to any action affecting the lands included in the trust and amendments to the Hawaiian Homes Commission Act that are enacted by the Hawaii State legislation affecting the beneficiaries under the Act;

- clarification that the Office of Native Hawaiian Relations within the U.S. Department of the Interior has the duty to consult with the Interagency Coordinating Group, other federal agencies, and the State of Hawaii on policies, practices, and proposed actions affecting Native Hawaiian resources, rights or lands;

- clarification that the section of S. 147 addressing the duties of the Office of Native Hawaiian Relations shall have no applicability to the Department of Defense or to any agency or component of the Department of Defense, but the Secretary of Defense may designate one or more officials as liaison to the Office;

- clarification that the duties of the Federal agency members of the Interagency Coordinating Group are to consult with the Native Hawaiian Governing Entity, through the coordination referred to in section 6(d)(1) of S. 147, but the consultation obligation established in this provision shall apply only after the satisfaction of all the conditions refereed to in section 7(c)(6);

- clarification that the provisions of S. 147 relating to the duties of the member federal agencies of the Interagency Coordinating Group shall have no applicability to the Department of Defense or to any agency or component of the Department of Defense, but that the Secretary of Defense may designate one or more officials as liaison to the Interagency Coordinating Group;

- clarification that not later than 180 days after the date of enactment of S. 147, the Secretary of the Interior shall appoint the members of the Commission in accordance with subparagraph (B) of section 7(b)(2), and that in making appointments to the Commission, the Secretary may take into consideration a recommendation made by any Native Hawaiian organization;

- clarification that rather than requiring that each member of the Commission be Native Hawaiian, that each member of the Commission shall demonstrate, as determined by the Interior Secretary, that he or she has not less than 10 years experience in the study and determination of Native Hawaiian genealogy, and an ability to read and translate into English documents written in the Hawaiian language;

- clarification that among the matters that can be the subject of negotiations amongst the United States, the State of Hawaii, and the Native Hawaiian Governing Entity are grievances regarding assertions of historical wrongs committed against Native Hawaiians by the United States or by the State of Hawaii;

- clarification that any governmental authority or power to be exercised by the Native Hawaiian Governing Entity which is currently exercised by the state or federal governments shall be exercised by the Native Hawaiian Governing Entity only as agreed to in negotiations pursuant to section 8(b)(1) of S. 147; and beginning on the date on which legislation to implement such agreement has been enacted by the U.S. Congress, when applicable, and by the State of Hawaii, when applicable, and that this includes any required modifications to the Hawaii State Constitution in accordance with the Hawaii Revised Statutes;

- with regard to claims, a clarification that nothing in S. 147 –
  o creates a cause of action against the United States or any other entity or person;
  o alters existing law, including existing case law, regarding obligations on the part of the United States or the State of Hawaii with regard to Native Hawaiians or any Native Hawaiian entity;
  o creates any obligations that did not exist in any source of Federal law prior to enactment of this Act; or
  o established authority for the recognition of Native Hawaiian groups other than the Native Hawaiian Governing Entity;

- with regard to the sovereign immunity of the United States and the State of Hawaii, provides that nothing in S. 147 is intended to create or allow to be maintained in any court any potential breach-of-trust actions, land claims, resource-protection or resource-management claims, or similar types of claims brought by or on behalf of Native Hawaiians or the Native Hawaiian governing entity for equitable, monetary, or Administrative Procedure Act-based relief against the United States or the State of Hawaii, whether or not such claims specifically assert an alleged breach of trust, call for an accounting, seek declaratory relief, or seek the recovery of or compensation for lands once held by Native Hawaiians;

- with regard to the establishment and retention of the sovereign immunity of the United States and the State of Hawaii, a clarification that to effectuate the ends expressed in section 8(c)(1) and 8(c)(2)(A), and that notwithstanding any other provision of Federal law, the United States retains its sovereign immunity to any claim that existed prior to enactment of S. 147, including but not limited to any claim based in whole or part on past events, and which could be brought by Native Hawaiians or any Native Hawaiian governing entity, and further providing that no pre-existing waiver of sovereign immunity, including but not limited to waivers set forth in chapter 7 of part I title 5, United States Code, and sections 1505 and 2409a of title 28, United States Code, shall be applicable to any such claims, and providing that this complete retention or reclaiming of sovereign immunity also applies to every claim that might attempt to rely on S. 147 for support, without regard to the source of law under which any such claim might be asserted;

- with regard to the effect of these provisions relating to claims and sovereign immunity, a clarification that it is the general effect of section 8(c)(2)(A), along with claims of a similar nature and claims arising out of the same nucleus of operative facts as could give rise to claims of the specific types referred to in section 8(c)(2)(A) be rendered nonjusticiable in suits brought by plaintiffs other than the federal government;

- with regard to the sovereign immunity of the State of Hawaii, clarification that notwithstanding any other provision of federal law, the State of Hawaii retains its sovereign immunity, unless waived in accord with state law, regarding Native Hawaiians, that existed prior to enactment of S. 147, and further providing that nothing in S. 147 is to be construed to constitute an override pursuant to section 5 of the Fourteenth Amendment of state sovereign immunity held under the Eleventh Amendment to the U.S. Constitution;

- clarification that the Native Hawaiian Governing Entity and Native Hawaiians may not conduct gaming activities either as a matter of claimed inherent authority or under the authority of any Federal law, including the Indian Gaming Regulatory Act, or under any regulations under that Act promulgated by the Secretary of the Interior or the National Indian Gaming Commission, and further providing that the foregoing prohibition apply regardless of whether gaming by Native Hawaiians or the Native Hawaiian governing entity would be located on land within the State of Hawaii or within any other state or territory of the United States;

- clarification that notwithstanding any other provision of law, including but not limited to part 151 of title 25, Code of Federal Regulations, the Secretary of the Interior shall not take land into trust on behalf of individuals or groups claiming to be Native Hawaiian or on behalf of the Native Hawaiian Governing Entity;

- clarification that the Indian Trade and Intercourse Act, 25 U.S.C. § 177, does not, has never, and will not apply after enactment of S. 147 to lands or land transfers present, past or future in the State of Hawaii, and further providing that if a court were to construe the Trade and Intercourse Act to apply to lands or land transfers in Hawaii before the date of enactment of S. 147, then any transfer of land or natural resources located within the State of Hawaii prior to the date of enactment of S. 147, by or on behalf of all the Native Hawaiian people, or individual Native Hawaiians, shall be deemed to have been made in accordance with the Indian Trade and Intercourse Act and any other provision of Federal law that specifically applies to transfers of land or natural resources from, by, or on behalf of an Indian tribe, Native Hawaiians, or Native Hawaiian entities;

- clarification that S. 147 will result in the recognition of a single Native Hawaiian Governing Entity, and that additional Native Hawaiian groups shall not be eligible for acknowledgment pursuant to the Federal Acknowledgment Process set forth in part 83 of title 25 of the Code of Federal Regulations or any other administrative or acknowledgment process;

- with respect to jurisdiction, clarification that nothing in S. 147 alters the civil or criminal jurisdiction of the United States or the State of Hawaii over the lands and persons within the State of Hawaii, and that the status quo of federal and state jurisdiction can change only as a result of further legislation, if any, enacted after the conclusion, in relevant part, of the negotiation process established in section 8(b);

- with regard to the eligibility of Native Hawaiians for federal programs and services provided to Indians because of their status under Federal law as Indians, clarification that notwithstanding section 7 (c)(6), because of the eligibility of the Native Hawaiian Governing Entity and its citizens for Native Hawaiian programs and services in accordance with subsection (g), nothing in S. 147 provides an authorization for eligibility to participate in any Indian program or service to any individual or entity not otherwise eligible for the program or service under applicable Federal law; and

- clarification that the Native Hawaiian governing entity and its citizens shall be eligible for Native Hawaiian programs and services to the extent and in the manner provided by other applicable laws.

Apology Resolution

PUBLIC LAW 103-150

To acknowledge the 100th anniversary of the Jan. 17, 1893,
overthrow of the Kingdom of Hawai'i, and to offer an apology to
Native Hawaiians on behalf of the United States for the
overthrow of the Kingdom of Hawai'i.
Signed by President William Clinton on Nov. 23, 1993

Public Law

103-150

In the Congress of the United States
Congressional Record, Vol. 139 (1993)
October 27, considered and passes Senate
November 15, considered and passes House

Calendar No. 185 103rd Congress 1st Session

Joint Resolution

To acknowledge the 100th anniversary of the January 17, 1893 overthrow of the Kingdom of
Hawai'i, and to offer an apology to Native Hawaiians on behalf of the United States for the
overthrow of the Kingdom of Hawaii.

Whereas, prior to the arrival of the first Europeans in 1778, the Native Hawaiian people lived in a highly organized, self-sufficient, subsistent social system based on communal land tenure with a sophisticated language, culture, and religion;

Whereas, a unified monarchical government of the Hawaiian Islands was established in 1810 under Kamehameha I, the first King of Hawaiʻi;

Whereas, from 1826 until 1893, the United States recognized the independence of the Kingdom of Hawaiʻi, extended full and complete diplomatic recognition to the Hawaiian Government, and entered into treaties and conventions with the Hawaiian monarchs to govern commerce and navigation in 1826, 1842, 1849, 1875, and 1887;

Whereas, the Congregational Church (now known as the United Church of Christ), through its American Board of Commissioners for Foreign Missions, sponsored and sent more than 100 missionaries to the Kingdom of Hawaiʻi between 1820 and 1850;

Whereas, on January 14, 1893, John L. Stevens (hereafter referred to in this Resolution as the "United States Minister"), the United States Minister assigned to the sovereign and independent Kingdom of Hawaiʻi conspired with a small group of non-Hawaiian residents of the Kingdom of Hawaiʻi, including citizens of the United States, to overthrow the indigenous and lawful Government of Hawaiʻi;

Whereas, in pursuance of the conspiracy to overthrow the Government of Hawaiʻi, the United States Minister and the naval representatives of the United States caused armed naval forces of the United States to invade the sovereign Hawaiian nation on January 16, 1893, and to position themselves near the Hawaiian Government buildings and the Iolani Palace to intimidate Queen Liliʻuokalani and her Government;

Whereas, on the afternoon of January 17, 1893, a Committee of Safety that represented the American and European sugar planters, descendants of missionaries, and financiers deposed the Hawaiian monarchy and proclaimed the establishment of a Provisional Government;

Whereas, the United States Minister thereupon extended diplomatic recognition to the Provisional Government that was formed by the conspirators without the consent of the Native Hawaiian people or the lawful Government of Hawaiʻi and in violation of treaties between the two nations and of international law;

Whereas, soon thereafter, when informed of the risk of bloodshed with resistance, Queen Liliʻuokalani issued the following statement yielding her authority to the United States Government rather than to the Provisional Government:

> *"I Liliʻuokalani, by the Grace of God and under the Constitution of the Hawaiian Kingdom, Queen, do hereby solemnly protest against any and all acts done against myself and the Constitutional Government of the Hawaiian Kingdom by certain persons claiming to have established a Provisional Government of and for this Kingdom.*
>
> *"That I yield to the superior force of the United States of America whose Minister Plenipotentiary, His Excellency John L. Stevens, has caused United States troops to be landed a Honolulu and declared that he would support the Provisional Government.*
>
> *"Now to avoid any collision of armed forces, and perhaps the loss of life, I do this under protest and impelled by said force yield my authority until such time as the Government of the United States shall, upon facts being presented*

to it, undo the action of its representatives and reinstate me in the authority
which I claim as the Constitutional Sovereign of the Hawaiian Islands.".
Done at Honolulu this 17th day of January, A.D. 1893.;

Whereas, without the active support and intervention by the United States diplomatic and military representatives, the insurrection against the Government of Queen Lili'uokalani would have failed for lack of popular support and insufficient arms;

Whereas, on February 1, 1893, the United States Minister raised the American flag and proclaimed Hawai'i to be a protectorate of the United States;

Whereas, the report of a Presidentially established investigation conducted by former Congressman James Blount into the events surrounding the insurrection and overthrow of January 17, 1893, concluded that the United States diplomatic and military representatives had abused their authority and were responsible for the change in government;

Whereas, as a result of this investigation, the United States Minister to Hawai'i was recalled from his diplomatic post and the military commander of the United States armed forces stationed in Hawai'i was disciplined and forced to resign his commission;

Whereas, in a message to Congress on December 18, 1893, President Grover Cleveland reported fully and accurately on the illegal acts of the conspirators, described such acts as an "act of war, committed with the participation of a diplomatic representative of the United States and without authority of Congress", and acknowledged that by such acts the government of a peaceful and friendly people was overthrown;

Whereas, President Cleveland further concluded that a "substantial wrong has thus been done which a due regard for our national character as well as the rights of the injured people requires we should endeavor to repair" and called for the restoration of the Hawaiian monarchy;

Whereas, the Provisional Government protested President Cleveland's call for the restoration of the monarchy and continued to hold state power and pursue annexation to the United States;

Whereas, the Provisional Government successfully lobbied the Committee on Foreign Relations of the Senate (hereafter referred to in this Resolution as the "Committee") to conduct a new investigation into the events surrounding the overthrow of the monarchy;

Whereas, the Committee and its chairman, Senator John Morgan, conducted hearings in Washington, D.C., from December 27,1893, through February 26, 1894, in which members of the Provisional Government justified and condoned the actions of the United States Minister and recommended annexation of Hawai'i;

Whereas, although the Provisional Government was able to obscure the role of the United States in the illegal overthrow of the Hawaiian monarchy, it was unable to rally the support from two-thirds of the Senate needed to ratify a treaty of annexation;

Whereas, on July 4, 1894, the Provisional Government declared itself to be the Republic of Hawai'i;

Whereas, on January 24, 1895, while imprisoned in Iolani Palace, Queen Lili'uokalani was forced by representatives of the Republic of Hawai'i to officially abdicate her throne;

Whereas, in the 1896 United States Presidential election, William McKinley replaced Grover Cleveland;

Whereas, on July 7, 1898, as a consequence of the Spanish-American War, President McKinley signed the Newlands Joint Resolution that provided for the annexation of Hawai'i;

Whereas, through the Newlands Resolution, the self-declared Republic of Hawaii ceded sovereignty over the Hawaiian Islands to the United States;

Whereas, the Republic of Hawai'i also ceded 1,800,000 acres of crown, government and public lands of the Kingdom of Hawai'i, without the consent of or compensation to the Native Hawaiian people of Hawai'i or their sovereign government;

Whereas, the Congress, through the Newlands Resolution, ratified the cession, annexed Hawai'i as part of the United States, and vested title to the lands in Hawai'i in the United States;

Whereas, the Newlands Resolution also specified that treaties existing between Hawai'i and foreign nations were to immediately cease and be replaced by United States treaties with such nations;

Whereas, the Newlands Resolution effected the transaction between the Republic of Hawai'i and the United States Government;

Whereas, the indigenous Hawaiian people never directly relinquished their claims to their inherent sovereignty as a people or over their national lands to the United States, either through their monarchy or through a plebiscite or referendum;

Whereas, on April 30, 1900, President McKinley signed the Organic Act that provided a government for the territory of Hawai'i and defined the political structure and powers of the newly established Territorial Government and its relationship to the United States;

Whereas, on August 21,1959, Hawai'i became the 50th State of the United States;

Whereas, the health and well-being of the Native Hawaiian people is intrinsically tied to their deep feelings and attachment to the land;

Whereas, the long-range economic and social changes in Hawai'i over the nineteenth and early twentieth centuries have been devastating to the population and to the health and well-being of the Hawaiian people;

Whereas, the Native Hawaiian people are determined to preserve, develop and transmit to future generations their ancestral territory, and their cultural identity in accordance with their own spiritual and traditional beliefs, customs, practices, language, and social institutions;

Whereas, in order to promote racial harmony and cultural understanding, the Legislature of the State of Hawai'i has determined that the year 1993, should serve Hawai'i as a year of special reflection on the rights and dignities of the Native Hawaiians in the Hawaiian and the American societies;

Whereas, the Eighteenth General Synod of the United Church of Christ in recognition of the denomination's historical complicity in the illegal overthrow of the Kingdom of Hawai'i in 1893 directed the Office of the President of the United Church of Christ to offer a public apology to the Native Hawaiian people and to initiate the process of reconciliation between the United Church of Christ and the Native Hawaiians; and

Whereas, it is proper and timely for the Congress on the occasion of the impending 100th anniversary of the event, to acknowledge the historic significance of the illegal overthrow of the Kingdom of Hawai'i, to express its deep regret to the Native Hawaiian people, and to support the reconciliation efforts of the State of Hawai'i and the United Church of Christ with Native Hawaiians;

Now, therefore, be it *Resolved by the Senate and House of Representatives of the United States of America in Congress assembled,*

SECTION 1. ACKNOWLEDGMENT AND APOLOGY.

The Congress -

(1) on the occasion of the 100th anniversary of the illegal overthrow of the Kingdom of Hawai'i on January 17, 1893, acknowledges the historical significance of this event which resulted in the suppression of the inherent sovereignty of the Native Hawaiian people;

(2) recognizes and commends efforts of reconciliation initiated by the State of Hawai'i and the United Church of Christ with Native Hawaiians;

(3) apologizes to Native Hawaiians on behalf of the people of the United States for the overthrow of the Kingdom of Hawai'i on January 17, 1893 with the participation of agents and citizens of the United States, and the deprivation of the rights of Native Hawaiians to self-determination;

(4) expresses its commitment to acknowledge the ramifications of the overthrow of the Kingdom of Hawai'i, in order to provide a proper foundation for reconciliation between the United States and the Native Hawaiian people; and

(5) urges the President of the United States to also acknowledge the ramifications of the overthrow of the Kingdom of Hawai'i and to support reconciliation efforts between the United States and the Native Hawaiian people.

SEC. 2. DEFINITIONS.

As used in this Joint Resolution, the term "Native Hawaiians" means any individual who is a descendent of the aboriginal people who, prior to 1778, occupied and exercised sovereignty in the area that now constitutes the State of Hawai'i.

SEC. 3. DISCLAIMER.

Nothing in this Joint Resolution is intended to serve as a settlement of any claims against the United States.

— Approved November 23, 1993

Speaker Biographies

Davelyn Noelani Kalipi

Davelyn Noelani Kalipi was born and raised in Hilo, Hawaii. She graduated with a bachelor's degree in Government & Politics/ Economics from George Mason University and a juris doctor from the National Law Center at George Washington University. Ms. Kalipi served in the United States Army Judge Advocate General's Corps from 1996 to 1999. Ms. Kalipi is licensed to practice law in Hawaii and the District of Columbia. Ms. Kalipi served as Senator Akaka's Counsel from 1999 to 2005 and advised him on legislative issues pertaining to Veterans' Affairs, Judiciary, Homeland Security, Armed Services, U.S. Territories and Pacific Islands, and Native Hawaiians. Ms. Kalipi was appointed Democratic Staff Director on the Senate Committee on Veterans' Affairs in February 2005.

H. Christopher Bartolomucci

A partner with Hogan & Hartson, Mr. Bartolomucci focuses on appellate and Supreme Court litigation and other litigation involving complex legal issues and issues of constitutional law. Mr. Bartolomucci served in the administration of President George W. Bush as associate counsel to the president from January 20, 2001, to August 15, 2003. While serving in the White House, he assisted the president in matters ranging from the selection of federal judges to the consideration of pardon requests. He also has served as counsel to the inspector general of the District of Columbia; associate special counsel to the Senate Whitewater Committee; and a Bristow Fellow in the Office of the Solicitor General of the U.S. Department of Justice. Mr. Bartolomucci holds a bachelor's degree, *summa cum laude*, from Dartmouth College, and graduated *cum laude* from Harvard Law School. In law school, Mr. Bartolomucci served as an editor of the *Harvard Law Review*. Following law school, he clerked for The Honorable William L. Garwood of the U.S. Court of Appeals for the Fifth Circuit.

H. William Burgess

H. William Burgess is an attorney in Hawaii. After graduating from the University of Virginia Law School in 1953, he enrolled in the U.S. Marine Corps from 1953 to 1958 as a fighter pilot and legal officer. Mr. Burgess then joined the law firm of Carlsmith & Carlsmith and then A. William Barlow. In 1965, Mr. Burgess opened his own law office, where he focused full time on business and real property litigation. From 1969 to 1972, he was the volunteer president of the Legal Aid Society. And in 1979, Burgess was one of the founders and first president of the Neighborhood Justice Center of Honolulu, now called the Mediation Center of the Pacific. In 1994, he retired from his practice and became a trustee for a Maui shopping center in Chapter 11 reorganization. In July 2000, in *Arakaki v. State of Hawaii*, Mr. Burgess challenged the requirement that the trustees of the Office of Hawaiian Affairs be of Hawaiian ancestry. In March 2002, in *Arakaki v. Lingle*, Mr. Burgess challenged the constitutionality of the Office of Hawaiian Affairs and the Hawaiian Homes Commission Act. Mr. Burgess is a member of the Grassroot Institute of Hawaii, a nonprofit organization that has gained prominence through its intense campaign to educate the public and Congress about the Native Hawaiian Government Reorganization Act

Gail Heriot

Ms. Heriot is a Professor of Law at the University of San Diego School of Law. Ms. Heriot was formerly Associate Dean for Academic Affairs & Professor of Law at George Mason University School of Law and Counsel to the Senate Judiciary Committee. She had a litigation practice as an associate at Hogan & Hartson, in Washington D.C. and Mayer, Brown & Platt at Chicago, Illinois. After graduating *cum laude* from the University of Chicago Law School, she served as a law clerk for the Honorable Seymour F. Simon of the Supreme Court of Illinois. She has numerous academic publications, such as: Faculty Editor for *A Symposium on Direct Democracy: An Introduction at the Journal of Contemporary Legal Issues*; *Standardized Tests under the Magnifying Glass: A Defense of the LSAT Against Recent Charges of Bias* at the TEXAS REVIEW OF LAW & POLITICS; and, *Strict Scrutiny, Public Opinion and Racial Preferences on Campus: Should the Courts Find a Narrowly Tailored Solution* at the HARVARD JOURNAL OF LEGISLATION.